"Make 'Em Well, Doc"

One Doctor's Journey from New Orleans to Baghdad and Back

—《《》》—

Jonathan D. Hunter, MD

TABLE OF CONTENTS

—⟨⟨⟨⟨⟩⟩⟩⟩—

v

———∞∞∞———

For Melissa, Grayson, and Avery.
You make me feel like a hero every day.

Foreword:

—⟨∅/∅⟩—

My earliest memory of Jonathan was a quick hello while passing between classes at Cavanaugh Hall on the Louisiana College Campus. I was accustomed to waking just in time to brush my teeth, pull on a semi-clean T-shirt, and slip into the class as the professor turned his back. Jonathan, on the other hand, was neatly dressed with the occasional cardigan, slacks, and loafers. His hair was neatly gelled and his ensemble was complemented by tiny, wire-framed glasses. I remember thinking "that guy has to be a pre-med major." It wasn't until a few weeks later that I met Jonathan through my future wife, Deanna, and her childhood friend, Melissa. Jonathan was "courting" Melissa at the time, and his execution in this endeavor was outstanding. I recall that he walked her to class every morning, rain or shine, for years. I must admit that I was not accustomed to hanging out with the guys I considered "brainy," but that all changed as I got to know Jonathan.

As Jonathan and I interacted more often, I found him to be rather interesting and not at all the person my first impression led me to assume. He was indeed one of those brainy guys, but there was so much more to him than a first glance would allow. In addition to being an outstanding student, he was confident, polite, and very outgoing. Over time, I began to admire many of his attributes and recognized the leadership potential this guy possessed.

We enjoyed the next few years at Louisiana College, occasionally hanging out and building a friendship. Jonathan participated in numerous extra-curricular activities while I concentrated on Officer Candidate School. Jonathan was always very supportive of my military career and made the trek to Camp Shelby, MS for my graduation and Commissioning Ceremony. He's always been one of those guys I could depend on.

Jonathan applied and was accepted to LSU Medical School in 1995. I must confess that I was very excited for him, although I knew that applying was merely a formality for this impressive fellow. It was commonplace for him to excel in any undertaking. A few years passed, we both married, and kept in touch as much as our schedules would allow. In 2000, Jonathan completed medical school and received his first choice to attend residency in Alexandria with LSU Family Practice. Needless to say, I was excited to have him within close proximity once again.

In early 2001 the National Guard was seeking physicians to support the Infantry Brigade in our state, and Jonathan instantly came to mind. I immediately called him and eagerly explained that he was exactly what the Guard needed. I knew he was the caliber leader we were looking for. He would soon prove to be a valuable officer and physician in our organization.

On May 15th, 2004 his Infantry Brigade was mobilized in Support of Operation Iraqi Freedom. Jonathan was called to active duty service. He arrived in Baghdad in late September 2004. To my knowledge, Jonathan was one of the few physicians to convoy humvee (HMMWV) with a combat unit from Kuwait to Baghdad. He served admirably as the Battalion Surgeon for 1/156th Armor Battalion, and earned the distinguished combat patches of the 256th Infantry Brigade and the 1st Cavalry Division. I later asked if he was upset with me for talking him into the National Guard. He exclaimed, "No, absolutely not, it is my pleasure and privilege to serve."

A few years have passed since we returned from the harsh environment of Baghdad, and our families have strengthened an already solid bond as a result. We regularly celebrate birthdays, holidays, tailgating at LSU football games, and other special occasions together. Our children have become close friends in the process. Uncle J, as he is affectionately known to my children, is "real fun and a pretty cool dude," according to them. He's always the life of the party and has become quite the chef over the years.

Above all that I respect and admire about Jonathan's character is his faith in God. He has been an example to all who know him, and he incorporates this faith into his daily walk. He is a man of integrity and it is evident through his actions. Others are drawn to him through his sincerity, compassion, and understanding. He is definitely fulfilling God's calling as a physician. I truly believe medicine is Jonathan's calling, and his conduit to touch others for God.

This is the character of the man I wish you to know. This writing gives a glimpse into the life of an extraordinary man I am proud to call friend. After many years, we still pass in the occasional hallway, Melissa is still the sparkle in his eyes, and the sharply dressed "brainy guy" of so many years ago has become a remarkable man.

Stuart West
Assistant S-3
Current Operations
256 IBCT

Preface

—◦◦◦—

This book is written for patients. Regardless of how "autobiographical" it may seem at times, my desire to bring this book to life was born out of an abiding desire to explain how my patients have blessed me as a physician. I was drawn to medicine out of a love for people and affinity for scientific fact. To me, medicine is a perfect marriage of my two deepest interests.

The road for me, as is often true for most physicians, has not always been easy. In fact, it has occasionally been downright treacherous. This book will detail paths in my life that literally have taken me through the "valley of the shadow of death." There have been lonely days and nights, weeks away from family, and moments of indescribable stress when the power of life and death rested in my hands alone. But it was in those times that God's peace rested with me and reminded me: I was placed here, at this very moment, to be his hand of healing to this very patient. They have been newborn babies, and they have been elderly adults suffering from Alzheimer's disease. They have been drug addicts and alcoholics in the emergency room. And they have been American soldiers.

Regardless of the difficulties I have encountered in this journey, it has been the passion of caring for them that pulls me out of bed each morning. Through my patients, I have found a daily renewal of my purpose on this earth, and this book is dedicated to them with all my thanks.

One

The Road Begins

—⸿⸿⸿—

I have always wanted to be a doctor. Many of my classmates in medical school and the undergraduates whom I would interview for acceptance arrived at the decision toward a career in medicine after long, introspective personal journeys. Mine was not such a journey.

I was born in Alexandria, Louisiana, on February 5, 1973, to two loving parents. Throughout my early years, the predominance of my social interaction, as an only child, was with adults. While I enjoyed my childhood friends immensely, my language skills flourished in long conversations with Mom and Dad about my favorite subjects: dinosaurs and insects. Before Steven Spielberg's *Jurassic Park* was ever conceived, I memorized such names as *Tyrannosaurus Rex, Ornitholestes, Dimetrodon,* and *Triceratops*. I captured insects in plastic cages and identified them in my field guide. I could not devour enough of these books, and I began reading at the age of three.

My academic success from elementary school years and beyond was born out of these two essential ingredients: a love for science and a precocious communicative ability. From the day I opened the Fisher Price Medical Kit—which is still available today, by the way—I wanted nothing more than to be a doctor when I grew up. As soon as I put the blood pressure cuff on Winnie the Pooh's arm, I was hooked. And I still am. My entire endeavor from then forward was driven at that aim—that one day, I would become a physician.

Of unequaled importance however, was my decision at age seven to place my trust in Jesus Christ. Despite the tenderness of my understanding, I could comprehend my need to reconcile myself to a perfect God, and in that pew at the First Baptist Church of Kingsville, Texas, Pastor Leslie Welch led me in prayer. From that day to this, God has walked with me through every step of my journey.

At the time of my graduation in June 1991 from Westerville North High School in Westerville, Ohio, both Mom and Dad were employees of The Ohio State University. Naturally, I gave careful consideration to attending OSU for a litany of good reasons: it was close to home, there were no barriers to any field of study in preparation for medical school, the scholarship possibilities were attractive, given my high school resume. But in the end, I did not even apply there.

After lengthy discussions with my family in the fall on 1990, I had decided to consider attending Louisiana College, in Pineville, Louisiana. Incidentally, Dad was the Director of Student Activities there when I was born, and my parents had always treasured the place. I could recall vague memories of our return visits there to check on friends they had made in the 70s, and we had lived there again briefly in the mid-80s. Nestled in a pine and dogwood grove in central Louisiana, L.C. was a Baptist liberal arts college of about a thousand students. This contrast to the behemoth that was Ohio State would actually end up easing my decision process. Dating back to the 1940s, L.C. had grown a reputation for unreal acceptance rates into medical school. At the time of my application, acceptance rates were approximately 90% — roughly double the national average. Not long after my application had been submitted, I was invited for a scholarship interview.

L.C. was a beautiful, warm place. Even though it was winter, the campus was still green and lush. The people were kind and genuine, and I instantly felt at home. Included was an informal interview with the pre-medical advisor and Professor of Biology, Dr. Joe B. Black. I was admittedly intimidated at the prospect of meeting this man, whom I had already learned was something of a legend in the region. Aside from being an accomplished researcher of crayfish genetics, he was known to be the man who put people into medical schools. He welcomed my parents and me warmly and took me into his personal lab to show me his research species. He was strikingly kind and humble, and amid his self-deprecating humor and 1950s-style flattop, I instantly loved him. I knew I had encountered more than a teacher and advisor. He would become a role model, mentor, and friend for years to come. With that, along with a generous scholarship offer, my decision was made. I could not have conceived how formative that decision would be.

And so as summer drew to a close, and my high school friends scattered off to Ohio State, Miami of Ohio, and Ohio University, I trekked south to Louisiana. As my parents drove away from Tudor Hall, the main men's dormitory, I knew the choice I had made would be far-reaching. Any co-dependence born out of 18 years as an only child would now be unraveled by a thousand miles of pure distance. Thankfully, I fell into a routine quickly: Invertebrate Biology, Honors English, and Western Civilization soon overwhelmed any twinges of homesickness. And while I was taking in xylem, phloem, and the Fertile Crescent [more to come later], I was somehow able to lobby enough votes to be elected Freshman Class President to the Student Government Association.

During this time, I met Melissa Ruth Cowart. While I had marched off to college with grand educational goals, I had also carried a pervasive desire to meet a beautiful Southern girl. I did just that one fateful Sunday night at the First Baptist Church of Pineville. Our friendship quickly blossomed—in no small part because of her pity for me being alone, so far from home—and friendship grew to something indescribably deeper. Despite the fact that we were each only 18 at the time, Melissa's influence was my ultimate maturing force. I knew then, as I still do now after 11 years of marriage, that she was God's daily presence in my life. So much of who I am today, I owe to her.

By my junior year of college, I was well-entrenched in the throes of Louisiana College's pre-med curriculum. Having survived the initial qualifying gauntlet of Dr. Dennis Watson's Chemistry 111 series, I had moved on to the most ominous adversary of any pre-med student: Organic Chemistry. Organic was a year-long course that met twice weekly—because it took all of the time in between to absorb the material! The laboratory portion met for three hours at a session, twice weekly, and was intended to materialize the electron football that was taught in lecture. Dr. Wayne McGraw, the legendary professor who had taught this course at L.C. for nearly 30 years, was nicknamed "Quick Draw" for his lightning-quick delivery style. It was my first glimpse into the future demands of medical school. Four-plus hours of study each night were necessary even to consider passing. I can recall the only interruption I permitted myself was "E.R." on Thursday nights. It seemed at the time that regardless of the drudgery of electrophilic aromatic substitution or alkene addition, I could break away for just an hour and imagine myself as one day being an actual Dr. Mark Green or John Carter.

It was during this year that I was introduced to someone who would become my first patient. At the time, she was a 20-year-old coed who had suffered from a fainting condition known as vasodepressor syncope. Despite having had thorough medical care, her passing out had continued to worsen, with spells occurring in increasing and debilitating frequency. She had been unable to obtain a driver's license and could go nowhere alone, for fear of another attack. Her medication dosing had subsequently been increased to a level where side effects were inevitably beginning to rival the actual illness itself! At the suggestion of the girl's father, who I had also come to know, I designed a research project framed around an exercise plan that would hopefully lead to fewer syncopal events and less need for medication. She was a trooper. Three to four times weekly, she would endure the combined torment of exercise and having a guy watch her do it! Week after week passed with lengthening intervals on the Schwinn Airdyne. As she tolerated more time on the bike, I would increase the intensity. In the end, our goals were realized. As her heart rates gradually slowed, she was able to reduce her initially whopping doses of beta-blockers, and her fainting virtually ceased. I felt like a miracle-worker. Big articles were written in the student newspaper and the yearbook, detailing the success of the project, and I was affirmed toward a career in medicine in a way I had never been previously.

If this had not been enough reinforcement of my direction in life, Jim Spencer, my pastor at the time, approached me about a medical mission trip opportunity to Córdoba, Mexico. Brother Jim's wife, Faye, had worked for years for a local ophthalmologist who took regular trips to Mexico to perform eye surgeries for the indigent—mostly cataract removals. This ophthalmologist, Dr. Tom Robinson, flew his own plane down multiple times a year and led a team of fellow eye surgeons in an intensive few days of virtually non-stop operations. There was obviously a great need for assistants to sterilize the equipment, perform visual measurements on patients, and first-assist with the actual surgeries. Brother Jim, knowing of my interest in the medical field, extended the invitation to go. I was delighted at the prospect and gladly accepted—what better way to spend a spring break!

Having lived in south Texas for several years as a child, I had always had this image of Mexico as largely an arid desert. Wrong. As we flew into Córdoba, the plush mountainous contrast to my misconception glared at me from every direction. With its extreme southeastern coastal location, Córdoba was temperate and green, serving as a major regional coffee and sugar producer. It was absolutely gorgeous. As we rode out the dirt road to the mission where we would be living and working for the next few days, I felt as if I had stepped off into a Mexican tourism commercial. The snow-capped volcano, *Pico de Orizaba*, loomed off in the distance, only transiently veiled by passing banana or mango trees. We had no sooner put down our luggage in the mission, however, than patients, having heard rumors of our arrival, began lining up at the gates.

The Córdoban people were as anciently beautiful as their homeland. Most were rather diminutive, with chiseled features and deep-set, black eyes: a look that belonged to an age long past. Unlike the cataracts of American patients, who typically undergo cataract removal at an earlier stage of progression, most of the cataracts we removed in Mexico were profoundly advanced—often to the point of causing blindness.

After our patients had been screened and measured for lens implants, they were prepped and underwent a local anesthetic injection. Under the surgical microscope, the dense, yellowed lens would be coaxed out and then replaced with the implant, for which they had been measured preoperatively. By that evening, vision that had been muted and blurry for years was suddenly brilliant. They would lie motionless on the table, suppressing any fear of the rows of tiny, sharp instruments around them. Despite knowing the sentence *"No se mueve,"* for "Don't move," I don't think I remember uttering it once. After all, those people were unspeakably grateful to be there. I saw many weeping as they left, hours before they would even experience the wonderful shock of their new sight. Later, the resident Southern Baptist missionary explained to me that the people looked upon the hands of our physicians as a healing touch from God Himself.

Dr. Robinson was one of those rare people who just oozed Christ in everything he did and said: humble, deliberate, and peaceful in even the tense situations I observed. Regardless of the circumstance, he wore the same wisp of a smile—like he knew something the rest of us didn't. By the end of the week, I was aware that the trip had less to do with life-altering ophthalmic surgery. Those doctors could have been patching leaky roofs; lives would have still been inexorably altered.

As Dr. Robinson's plane lifted off the ground, I was too moved to be tired. Had I been *completely* uninterested in medicine, I would have still been gripped by the protracted display of greatness I had witnessed: awe-inspiring people affecting earthly and eternal significance in those who needed it most.

As my college years drew to a close, Melissa and I decided to marry after my graduation. With one year remaining in her degree program, I planned to work for a year while applying to medical school. My first job out of college would be as an admissions counselor at L.C., covering the recruiting territory throughout south Louisiana. I was thrilled—not just to have a job—but to be paid to travel around what I deemed to be the most colorful, intriguing part of the state. This territory stretched from Lake Charles across Lafayette, to include the greater New Orleans area. For most of the fall, I stayed on the road, going to high school programs to promote the college I had come to love.

My most cherished trips were to New Orleans. Admittedly, the Big Easy had intimidated me. After living in serene little Pineville for the past four years, I was not accustomed to traffic or the threat of crime. Yet as often happens to visitors of "the city that care forgot," I developed a profound affinity for this truly unique American city. Foremost among the reasons were its people. New Orleaneans are a people with a heritage unlike any other, with immigrant roots derived from Creole slaves, Italians, Croatians, and of course, the French. The lauded food, architecture, and music are all offspring of this amazing cultural amalgam, and I couldn't get enough of it.

By November, I had received an invitation to interview at Louisiana State University's School of Medicine in New Orleans. This was great news. Since medical schools will typically fill the next year's class as the interview season progresses, an earlier interview typically carries a greater chance of acceptance. My three interviews went well, each being calm and conversational. I wore a red paisley bowtie in the hope that it would make me a bit more memorable to the admissions committee. It worked.

Melissa called me at work to let me know that The Envelope had come in the mail—and that it was thick. I raced home so we could open it together. The enclosed letter from Dr. John Ruby, the Associate Dean for Admissions, read as follows:

December 14, 1995

Dear Mr. Hunter,

On behalf of the Committee on Admissions, I am pleased to offer you a position in the first year class at the Louisiana State University School of Medicine in New Orleans for the 1996 academic year...

We sat there on the borrowed sofa in our rented shotgun house and embraced.

Two

This Is Not College

—◁◈◈◈▷—

Most medical education begins its training year in July, so little time elapsed between Melissa's graduation and our move from Pineville to New Orleans. She had triumphantly secured a position with the St. Charles Parish School Board and would be teaching middle school special education in one of the state's finest programs. So in June of 1996, we emptied our one-bedroom shotgun house into a utility truck and headed southeast.

The Louisiana State University School of Medicine has historically been synonymous with Charity Hospital of New Orleans. With roots actually going back to the early eighteenth century, Charity was begun to fulfill the same mission that it has lately: to provide medical care to the sizeable indigent population of New Orleans. Its present location was completed in 1939 under the direction of the magnanimous Governor Huey P. Long, and was the second largest hospital in America, bearing a capacity of 3,300 patients. By the time I arrived on the scene, however, "Big Charity" was a hulking relic of populism. Internal medicine, obstetrics, pediatrics, and a considerable amount of surgery had already been moved down the street to University Hospital. Yet, passing through its massive front doors into its grand entry, flanked by paintings of giants like Dr. Rudolph Matas and Sister Stanislaus, anyone would know that they were in a hallowed place. The first day of medical school was a blur of introductory speeches in the first-year lecture hall at the Medical Education Building a few blocks from Charity. Department heads, the Dean, and even the Chancellor filed in and out to welcome the roughly 170 of us.

The one address that I can clearly recall was given by the course director for Gross Anatomy, Dr. William Swartz. He was introduced by the Associate Dean and as he strode forward from the back of the hall, the large room fell silent. Gross anatomy, as is often the case for all first-year medical students, was the hub for everything that would be learned in the first semester. "Gross," as it is affectionately called, is the first great test of one's ability to negotiate the challenges of medical education. Among these are: the demand of memorizing hundreds of structures, locations, and functions of every conceivable muscle, nerve, artery, organ, bone, dissecting cooperatively with three other "partners" in the lab, and, of course, standing daily for hours over a dead body! Dr. Swartz took the lapel microphone from the Associate Dean, stared up at us for few seconds, and proclaimed in his upper Midwest accent, *"This is nat callege."* And so it began.

I would later learn that my first patient in medical school had been a retired retail employee at a department store in Baton Rouge. Before he had succumbed to congestive heart failure, he had elected to donate his body to medical science—donation in the truest sense, as no payment is legally permitted. I met my three partners with whom I would be sharing dissection for the next five months, and we were given instructions to roll the cadaver over and begin dissection on the back. The back is the typical starting point for new students because of its ease of access, as well as its low technical demand.

Within minutes, a thud echoed across the lab as we had suffered our first "casualty." Passing out is not terribly uncommon on the first day: between the sight of the body, the burning smell of the formalin preservative, and the sheer experience of rolling over a dead body, a whopping sensory overload is often the result. Even before we had recovered from our downed comrade, I heard a blurted expletive behind me as another of my classmates had jammed the broad no. 10 scalpel blade into her palm. It cuts well.

And so the weeks plowed along. With each passing day, my patient revealed a little more about the marvels of the human body. Dissection of the back and upper extremity gave way to the head and neck with its astoundingly intricate network of nerves and vessels. Hour after hour would be spent in that 55-degree lab, leaning over an area the size of a square inch. When we weren't in the gross lab, we were in lecture: soaking up the physiology, cell biology, and embryology that paralleled the present focus in anatomy. Then study. Deep into the night—every night—I could be found at the kitchen table, treading water until the next day, when more information would be added to the "stack." By the time the test rolled around, covering every subject over the previous six weeks, my study notes looked like a New York phone book. Somehow, we survived.

The second semester brought on the study of disease, after the foundation of normal anatomy and physiology had been placed. Pathology, immunology, parasitology, and biochemistry even exceeded the pace maintained by the first semester! Yet it was during this tumult that I acquired my first *living* patient relationship since starting medical school. Traditionally, medical education in America was framed around a sharp divide between the first two pre-clinical years and the last two years, which were purely clinical. The basis for this structure was simply based on the belief that the clinical experience would be meaningless without a thorough basic science foundation.

At the time I began in 1996, however, an effective push was sweeping the country to begin inclusion of clinical experiences as early as the first and second years. Education experts agreed, as did most young physicians, that the earlier introduction of carefully selected patient encounters humanized the first two years. In the end, what was hopefully produced was a better-rounded, patient-oriented doctor with a deeper, practically reinforced fund of knowledge. Yet there must at least be some basic knowledge in place prior to these events or, as was so aptly stated to us by anatomy professor and Associate Dean for Admissions Dr. Sam McClugage, "It's just entertainment."

The aforementioned patient was the result of an assignment in the Introduction to Clinical Medicine course. We would crawl before walking, assigned merely to go conduct a history on an inpatient at University Hospital. The history that a doctor takes from any patient is essentially the interrogatory that, if thoroughly performed, will often reveal the diagnosis without even lifting a stethoscope. Which was a good thing, because I was not yet "stethoscope-capable"! My patient was a 53 year-old African-American male suffering from the profound and multiple complications of AIDS. Chief among these was an Alzheimer's-like dementia that had virtually incapacitated him intellectually.

I knew the history would be difficult when I had to wake him from a deep sleep. He was gaunt and wasted, and his half-open eyes were in another place. It required all of his scant strength to merely sit up in the sweaty sheets. I began my questions, conjoined to the spiral-bound reference cards I had bought at the campus bookstore.

"Are you having any insomnia?"

"Do you use drugs? Which ones?"

"Do you have sex with men, women, or both?"

I was embarrassingly wooden and awkward, cringing with each question, knowing how ridiculous I must have sounded. The poor man would garble a response and I scratched some notes, hoping that I would somehow be able to translate it later. Every few questions, he would slide back into his medicated slumber, and I would have to rouse him again. An excruciating hour later, I relieved him of my novice presence. He fell back asleep, and I slunk down the hall and back to my books.

Astoundingly, after my humbling experience with the history, later that week I leaped at an elective clinical rotation in geriatrics. We would be given a patient at a nursing facility in the nearby neighborhood known as Mid-City. By then, I had thankfully acquired a few more history-taking skills since my prior debacle. My assigned patient was a lady of 73. Unlike before, when I walked into her room, I found a patient alert, dressed, and sitting in a recliner, watching *Days of Our Lives*. I was thrilled. My initial line of questioning was purely conversational as I attempted to establish some rapport with her. She was a lifelong resident of New Orleans with parents of Italian descent. She was a retired seamstress and had two children: one in Chicago and the other still in New Orleans. Yet as my line of questioning progressed to more current matters, she became oddly defensive. Despite taking a literal list of medications, she denied any medical problems whatsoever. When I inquired into the current month, she claimed that she didn't keep up with that anymore.

This would be the first of countless encounters I would have with the hateful entity known as Alzheimer's disease. As with all similar patients, the recent memories and complex processing capabilities wane first. Then, as the condition inevitably progresses, distant memories fade as well. Eventually, all interpersonal recognition and interactive ability slip down the same black hole. As Nancy Reagan so aptly described, it is indeed "the long goodbye."

I continued my weekly visits with my little friend in Mid-City for the remainder of the semester. Each week when I arrived, I had to reintroduce myself and tell her why I was there. Today in my practice, I see Alzheimer's patients almost daily. I have no doubt that my tenderness toward these precious patients and their families was born out of this formative experience.

Toward the end of the exhausting second year of medical school, we were all eager to exchange the books and volumes of notes for the short white coats of the third year. I would start with surgery. Wow.

By July of 1998, Melissa and I had an eight-month-old baby girl. She grew increasingly inter-active, and I enjoyed every second of her coos and giggles.

The first component of my surgical rotation would be at the VA Hospital of New Orleans, a mammoth structure looming in the shadow of Charity Hospital. To permit myself enough time to see all of my assigned patients before rounds at 6:00am, I would routinely leave by 4:00. Like most patients in a large regional medical center, mine were the sickest of the sick. Aggressive diagnoses like necrotizing pancreatitis, Fournier's gangrene, and sigmoid volvulus were present simultaneously in the surgical intensive care unit. Our responsibility was to examine our patients and then document an extensive note detailing the events of the previous day. Key points such as drain output, presence of fever and how high, and whether or not the patient was passing gas were all expected on request from the surgical residents. Alas, these poor residents were generally not warm folks.

Before the Accreditation Council for Graduate Medical Education limited residents to an 80-hour week, physicians-in-training typically were exceeding 100 hours. With this pace, aside from the prevalent quality of care issues, residents were chronically fatigued and irritable. The excessive hours, combined with the inherent stressors of life-and-death decision making, yielded two-legged monsters in white coats. That's what we got. It was unfortunate that much of our apprehension regarding our surgical rotation had in fact been realized: malignant masses combined with malignant personalities.

Yet, as always, the patients redeemed the experience. That and some really dynamic faculty. I somehow found a swift affinity for the VA patients. They all had a story—that they were usually quite willing to relate—about their particular combat experience and how it profoundly related to current events. Most of the men I treated were WWII veterans with a smattering of pony-tailed Vietnam vets. Whether it was Normandy or the Mekong Delta, I learned all that I could from them—while whacking away at their skin cancers or changing their wound dressings.

On a rotating basis, the students would take turns "scrubbing in" to the operating room. I was always ambivalent about this. While the surgeries were often fascinating, medical students were typically relegated to standing at the end of the table, out of sight of the procedure, or they were given retraction duty: holding unrelated things out of the way so that related things could be fixed. All the while, the student must be prepared for the volleyed question about anatomic structure or surgical concept.

One particular morning as I scrubbed in, I learned that Dr. J. Patrick O'Leary, Chair of the Department of Surgery at LSU, would be supervising the case. This was quite an event. The residents started the partial hemicolectomy as I assumed my obligatory position at the end of the operating table. Five minutes later, O'Leary backed into the O.R., greeting everyone as he was gowned by the nurse. He took his position next to the third-year resident as the abdominal cavity was entered. Immediately at that point he inquired, "Who's my student down there?" Cold sweat.

"Get up here, Jonathan. I want to show you something."

The resident obliged the change of positions as Dr. O'Leary asked me the three main divisions of the celiac artery.

"Left gastric, common hepatic, and splenic," I answered affirmatively.

"Correct. Now," with his right hand deep in the incision, "slip your hand right here over mine, and I'm going to feed you the spleen."

As his hand pulled away, the smooth warmth of the man's spleen dropped right into my palm—not a thing like the pickled version I had encountered in gross anatomy. It was amazing…but not enough to make me want to go into surgery.

We moved on from the inpatient surgical experience to mini rotations through its various subspecialties. My first two weeks would be spent with the plastic surgery fellows: breast reductions, skin grafts, and cleft palate repairs would replace the gall bladders and hernias of the VA. One afternoon of particular significance, September 13, 1998, I found myself in the plastic surgery clinic, high in the stratosphere at Charity. It was the first instant when I would observe a doctor cuss *at* a patient. The unfortunate gentleman had recently undergone a skin graft to the tip of his nose after removal of a cancerous growth and was at the clinic for the first postoperative check. The tenuous circumstances there revolved around the inherently stingy blood supply at the nasal tip, as well as the guy's three-pack-per-day smoking habit. Despite clear instructions otherwise, he had continued smoking in the interim, further compromising oxygen to the graft site. When I removed the dressings, instead of a beefy pink graft, there was only a shriveled raisin. The fellow who had worked so meticulously on that nose was livid, and communicated this to the patient in a manner unsuitable for public consumption.

As I lurked in the corner of the exam room, taking in the reprimand, I could hear thunder rolling outside with increasing frequency. That day, the eastern edge of Tropical Storm Frances was moving through the New Orleans area, and heavy rain was forecasted. As all of America knows by now, the Crescent City rests in a bowl between Lake Ponchartrain and the Mississippi River. Water drainage is accomplished against gravity via a pump-and-canal system that shunts water out of the city—at a maximum rate of about six-tenths of an inch per hour back then. As I peered out of the clinic window, I realized these limitations. Water was clearly over the sidewalks as far as I could see. By the time I left the clinic at 5:30, water was three feet high in every direction, and my only choice was to wade to my car, parked in a slightly more elevated lot four blocks away. As I sloshed down Claiborne Avenue, two blocks from the infamous Louisiana Superdome, cars that had earlier been parked on the street were actually banging against parking meters in the wakes of passing trucks. Thankfully, my car was only in a foot of water, and I was able to creatively navigate home. But that was not the last time I would observe waves in the shadow of the Superdome.

Not long after the conclusion of plastic surgery, I was commuted to Obstetrics, where I did my part in maintaining the population of greater New Orleans. Medical students were given the privilege of actually delivering the baby with the resident's supervision. And I delivered—a lot. Thankfully, unlike some of my classmates, I didn't drop one.

OB-GYN served as an ideal transition to pediatrics. If anything, I was delighted to be working with pediatric residents, who were almost by definition warm, fuzzy types. But I also loved treating kids. After the trenches of the VA surgical wards and the delivery rooms at University, I was ready for a change of pace. I began at Children's Hospital of New Orleans on the Hematology-Oncology floor. Children's was a real "Orleanean" facility, nestled in the oaks and mansions of the Garden District. Blocks away were Tulane University, Audubon Park, and the famed Commander's Palace restaurant. Like most academically affiliated hospitals of this type, it maintained a regional role in the treatment of all types of childhood diseases—even malignant ones.

The fourth floor at Children's was designated specifically for these patients: kids with acute myelogenous leukemia, astrocytoma, and Wilm's tumors, among many. My faculty were Drs. Lolie Yu and Raj Warrior: both internationally revered throughout their professions as eminent practitioners who loved kids. Like images seen from high visibility programs like St. Jude's, treatment of childhood malignancy is permeated by a spirit of optimism and hope. In spite of the little bald heads and pale faces, I soon learned that God has imbued us all with an inherent sense of determination in the face of struggle. Thankfully, I observed more success than failure during my rigorous weeks spent there, but beyond the relationship between "asparaginase and anaphylaxis," I left knowing more about courage.

My patients took a sudden burst in stature, as I concluded my rewarding pediatrics experience and moved back downtown for psychiatry. The third floor of Charity Hospital was—at that time—a locked unit for inpatient psychiatric treatment: as always, the sickest of the sick. I was buzzed into the unit on the morning of my first day to look over into the dayroom and witness a patient singing "Blue Suede Shoes" while he urinated on the wall. Our responsibility was to meet and interview an allotment of patients, and then report to the multidisciplinary team that met daily. The interview, beyond the initial small talk, included questions meant to assess their overall status and response to medications:

"Are you hearing voices?"

"Do you have any special powers?"

"What does 'People who live in glass houses shouldn't throw stones,' mean to you?"

Their responses were as unpredictable as they were fascinating. There were no R.P. McMurphy and Nurse Ratched cinematic moments, but I enjoyed it tremendously, and left with abiding interest in behavioral medicine. It's a good thing I did.

My final and most formative major rotation of the third year was Internal Medicine. Covering all of non-surgical adult medicine and its subspecialties, "medicine," as it is referred to, is absolutely central to the clinical experience. Internists are the masters of diagnosis. Through comprehensive history-taking and keen physical diagnostic skills, they deduce diagnoses based on a differential of possibilities. Regardless of a young physician's eventual choice of specialty, each carries vital skills endowed by the internists under whom they studied. Imagine the blessing when those teachers are among the finest in all of medical education.

Dr. Charles Sanders, Chair of LSU's Department if Internal Medicine and Dr. Fred Lopez, Coordinator of the Student Rotation, were both faculty respected far from the borders of the Crescent City. Not only were they just astonishingly great infectious disease specialists, but they were uniquely and genuinely interested in their students. On arriving in the department, Dr. Sanders would meet with each student to learn of his background, current interests, and future goals. This information would then be recorded in the "people file" he kept in his office. Not since Louisiana College had I encountered faculty with this degree of position-indifferent humility.

Dr. Lopez, though just an assistant professor at the time and not long out of his own fellowship, had already established the same reputation. We all had a small group meeting with Dr. Lopez, wherein he unraveled the complexities of acid-base balance—and gave blow-pops for correct answers. Time spent on rounds with these men yielded one revelation after the next: scant coloration of a fingernail or subtle characteristics of a heart murmur were used to guide the team right to an obscure diagnosis. In a particular case, we had recently admitted a 24-year-old Honduran man who had stowed away in a shipping freighter to gain entrance into the U.S. He had apparently suffered a devastating case of rheumatic fever as a child, most likely due to untreated strep throat. The impact of this illness, as was true in his case, is realized in heart valve damage. His was severe. All of his valves were profoundly affected, resulting in a hugely dilated heart that was unable to meet its demands. Dr. Sanders knew only his presenting symptoms at the time of the exam I witnessed. As he placed the head of his antiquated stethoscope on the man's chest, he closed his eyes. In 15 seconds, he opened his eyes and identified every single valve abnormality.

"Did he have rheumatic fever as a child?"

We all laughed. Was this guy good, or what?

About this time, I had the one lunch encounter that would instantly change my course of direction after medical school. Until then, with obviously seminal experiences in internal medicine, I had trained my sights on a possible career in cardiology. I was enthralled with the intellectual gymnastics of adult medicine, and dating back to my undergraduate days, was captivated by the heart. Still, I wasn't yet completely convinced that this was the right fit for me. Out of a voracious demand for family physicians, LSU had started a family medicine residency in Alexandria in 1997—right across the Red River from Pineville and Louisiana College. Dr. Dennis LaRavia was the charismatic founding director of the program and had come to New Orleans to recruit from our class. When the phrase "...could sell an Eskimo as ice cream freezer..." was established, I think it was done after Dr. LaRavia had been to Alaska.

He began the lunch with a prayer [unusual for a state school] and proceeded to rattle off all of the procedures taught in Alexandria as a means of equipping the modern family physician: colonoscopy, cardiac stress testing, dermatologic surgery with plastics repairs, vasectomy, nasolaryngoscopy. All of this training, combined with a holistic, psychosocial approach to the patient, appealed to my deepest draw toward medicine. That would prove to be one of my more formative lunch experiences!

During my fourth and final year of medical school, I was selected to serve as a student member of the Admissions Committee at LSU. In what I considered to be a singular honor, I would interview applicants and contribute to the selection process for the upcoming class. The fundamental mission of these committees is to sift through the reams of credentials and identify future physicians—not just academicians. Not surprisingly, all interviewees espoused broadly altruistic reasons for pursuing a career in medicine, and this served as a continuous reminder to me as I considered my choice of specialty. The love of people and the desire to build relationships with them through the healing process were inescapable. In the end, the decision was not difficult.

"Match Day" is the announcement date in March when all senior medical students in America discover where they will be performing their residency training. In a nutshell, students interview at programs of interest—in the specialty of their choosing—submitting a preference that ranks their choices. These respective programs then also rank their applicants in order of preference. A computer "matches" the lists and presto: Match Day.

By March of 2000, I had enjoyed a gratifying senior year. In addition to the required curriculum, I had taken electives in child sexual abuse and geriatrics. I had performed an acting internship in pediatrics back at Children's, savoring my first whiffs of autonomy: being on call, writing admission orders and discharge summaries, even writing prescriptions. Not surprisingly, I had decided to perform my required family medicine rotation at the LSU program in Alexandria. It was exactly the affirming experience that I had hoped it would be. Each day, I observed the care of patients from birth to death. In one room, I would be assisting in a circumcision and the next, discussing end-of-life issues with a family — all of this under the care of the most amazing single group of faculty I could have asked for. My decision was made. On March 16, 2000, with my two year-old daughter Grayson on one arm, I opened my envelope. There were no surprises. We were going back home to central Louisiana.

Three

Tempered

—◦◦◦—

Despite our love of New Orleans and its people, Melissa and I were delighted to return to Alexandria. After four years of traffic and bustle, we were all too ready to forego the land of food and jazz for a more relaxed pace. My fellow seven residents and I received a rock star welcome with a huge reception, media coverage, and gifts from the community. I was grateful that two of my medical school classmates, Mark Schneider and Lee Ellender, matched to Alexandria with me, carrying some sense of familiarity with me into this new environment. We each were cloaked with a set of new starched white coats—the long kind this time—and we set out on the next three years of on-the-job training.

Residency, regardless of specialty, is the experience during which medical students actually learn how to be doctors. Instead of the largely didactic methods of medical school, residency is essentially an intensive apprenticeship that imparts practice-relative skills in actual patient care. As I was actually told by a professor during one of my own medical school interviews, medical school provides "just enough knowledge to make you dangerous." I had sort of considered it in a "Conan-esque" manner, tempering the skills forged in med school. (I have always loved that metaphor!) Family medicine residencies bear the considerable burden of crafting the doctor who can deal with everything from womb to tomb. Whether providing care alone, or in concert with consulting specialists, the modern family doc is the first line of prevention and treatment of the disease process. We would rotate monthly through a prescribed curriculum of primary and specialty care while maintaining a clinic practice of continuity patients. Even though we might be off doing obstetrics or cardiology or dermatology, the consistent thread of the continuity clinic would remain. Patients I would see there would be mine throughout residency, forming the longitudinal relationship that is so fundamental to our specialty.

My fellow residents and I all agreed the faculty was the prime drawing factor to the LSU program at Alexandria. In keeping with most family physicians, they were all kind people with outstanding relational abilities. Some had years of private practice experience, and others were not long out of their own training programs. It was a great mix. And they were all Christians. Indeed, I knew that I was exactly where God had intended me to be.

Like all residencies, ours began July 1st. After we had been paraded around the local hospitals and rehabilitation facilities, it was time to get to work. I very quickly drew my first call night. When on call, the first year residents—or more commonly "interns"—would stay in the hospital all night while carrying the infamous Pager. It was our broad responsibility to answer all after-hours calls for medical advice or prescriptions, along with responding to any adult inpatient needs at the hospital. Considering that the program housed some 30 physicians, the amount of calls was formidable. One minute, there could be a call for a refill of blood pressure pills, and the next, there could be a patient arresting in the hospital.

My first night on call, I clipped the Pager to my belt and felt as if I had just taken possession of the nuclear launch code briefcase. I recall that it had three notification settings: audible, vibrate, and visceral fear. I selected all three. First-time mothers would call frequently—and for everything; I recall one panicked mom calling because her baby had just been bitten by a mosquito. Elderly patients would call with more alarming complaints as advanced medical conditions began deteriorating at home. Shortness of breath, chest pain, blood sugars of 450 were all commonplace. Despite having a great medical school experience, most rookie interns are rather uncomfortable with making medical decisions alone. Even though an upper level resident and a faculty member were always on backup call, the intern was tasked with providing the initial response.

In keeping with the physician's expected air of omniscience, most interns will devise any number of misdirection tactics to avoid the unthinkable. "Hmm...that's a good question. I really don't know the answer to that." I became quite proud of my own stall techniques, and actually taught them to junior residents when I later became Chief. With my reference books positioned strategically by the phone, I quickly grew proficient at extending the line of questioning—sometimes really extending it—while I looked up the answer.

And if the books didn't hold the answer, I had to pull out the big gun: "You know, there are several options for treating that condition. Let me run this by my supervising upper level, and I'll call you right back." In the end, I could nearly always cloak my cluelessness!

If the poor intern were sill alive by 7:00am the following morning, the Pager would be proudly handed off to the inpatient team for that day. War stories of intubations, cardiac arrests, and critical admissions to the ICU were traded—along with a Barney Fife snort and hitch of the pants.

I must confess that despite the intimidating learning curve associated with residency training, I was very happy. Unlike my poor medical school classmates, off being abused in some gargantuan medical center, I was being mentored in a truly nurturing environment. Unlike many residencies, where interns are looked upon as an indentured work force, our faculty actually cared about our personal welfare. Patient care was administered in a manner that took into account our development, as well as treatment of the patient, and I was deeply grateful for that. Indeed, it was a blessing to be surrounded by role models like so many I had known in medical school, and their example would serve my patients for years to come.

Family medicine interns are required to spend at least one half-day per week in the continuity clinic. My first patient would be memorable. I was hoping for something painless to gradually ease me into this new experience: a common cold or a high blood pressure follow-up, maybe. Not quite. As I heaved the chart from the door holder, its thickness immediately told me that this would not be easy. The patient was a middle-aged lady who was normally cared for by one of the faculty members. She had a remote history of a complex back surgery that had been unsuccessful due to anesthesia-related complications. If this weren't enough, she was now suffering from a deteriorating global neurologic condition similar to multiple sclerosis.

Consequently, she was nearly bed-ridden, except for her frequent doctor visits. Her initial difficulty with ambulating was beginning to extend to all of her motor functions. As I leaned into the room, I could immediately tell she was sick beyond her typically poor baseline. She was slumped down in her wheelchair as if she had lost the energy to exist. Her husband provided me with most of the history related to the preceding few days of abruptly declining energy and appetite, and I attempted to corroborate this while I examined her. I felt desperate pity for both of them. As I left the exam room to discuss it with the precepting faculty member, I was at a loss. Once again, was I ever thankful for the faculty in Alexandria as I sat down with Dr. Michael Madden to go through the entire history and physical.

After what must have been ten minutes, there was a pause, and then he asked me, "So what do you think we should do?"

This is where residency training takes a sharp divergence from medical school: instead of merely gathering information, the resident employs the information to make decisions. My first patient in the clinic was an admission to the hospital.

From this illustrious beginning, I began accumulating an incredible arsenal of clinical skills, both cognitive and procedural. As the weeks progressed, I became increasingly comfortable with adjusting diabetic medications in one room and doing a routine pediatric appointment in the next. When I delivered a baby boy in obstetrics, I was performing his circumcision shortly thereafter. I was now the only doctor in the room when life began and when it ended. Everything that I had imagined in that fateful lunch meeting not so long ago was taking shape, and I couldn't be happier.

We began residency in the throes of the 2000 presidential campaign. Although I had not ever been overly drawn to politics, I had always felt an abiding draw toward eventual public service. While unable to identify any particular avenue, I believed it to be a natural offspring of a career in medicine. I watched the coverage closely as the race neared, then became rabidly occupied with it during the hanging chad calamity in Florida. I was rotating through obstetrics at the time and would dart into the lounge between deliveries to catch the latest updates. Like many Americans at the time, I was hoping for a marked change of direction from the previous eight years and was elated with the eventual result. I happened to be on call January 20, 2001—Inauguration Day. Thankfully, circumstances were providentially ordained in the hospital to allow me 30 minutes to watch the coverage. That 30 minutes provided me the singular portion of the inaugural address that would be most meaningful. After being sworn in, President Bush, his voice shaking with emotion, through a drizzling rain asked Americans to "seek a common good beyond your comfort, to serve your nation, beginning with your neighbor...I ask you to be citizens: citizens, not spectators..." The familiar chime of the Pager beckoned, and I rushed off to the emergency room downstairs.

The following week, my friend, Stuart West called me at home. I had known Stuart since our days at Louisiana College, and he had married Melissa's childhood friend, Deanna. Stuart was also an Army National Guardsman. He had participated in the Guard all through college, and we had recently attended his commissioning ceremony after completion of officer candidate school. He was more than just a dear friend; I admired Stuart. I could immediately tell that he was anxious to talk to me about something that day, and he got right to it: "J, [my friends' moniker for me] have you ever thought about joining the Guard?"

He proceeded to detail the Army's recruitment and incentive program for physicians, going through each component and answering my preliminary questions. There were considerable monthly stipends or student loan repayment—all for an occasional weekend and two weeks in the summer. Melissa and I began serious discussion about this opportunity. Beyond the obvious financial benefit during residency, I would have a chance to serve my state and country, and fulfill an amorphous ambition that I had carried for so long. My grandfather was a WWII veteran, and my dad had served in Vietnam. In some way, I felt obliged to continue this proud tradition.

After weeks of phone conversations with Louisiana's Army Medical Department recruiter and completion of reams of forms, I was instructed to report to the military entrance processing station (MEPS) in Shreveport. MEPS facilities are tasked with determining a recruit's aptitude for military service via physical and cognitive testing. After getting lost once, I arrived there at 4:40am—ten minutes late. Taking a seat in the initial briefing room, I felt as if I were surrounded by children. Even though I was only 28 myself, the average Army recruiting age is 21. (It must have been 17 *that* day!) The noncommissioned officer in charge of the station then proceeded with the initial orientation. I was amazed—why, I don't know—at the paternalistic nature of this orientation: "Do not pick up your pencil until instructed to do so...If you must use the restroom, you must ask permission...There is no food or drink allowed in this building." And so I proceeded with the litany of blood tests, urine drug screening, and an extensive physical exam. At the end of the morning, I got back in my car and drove away. The recruits who were at MEPS with me were swearing in as I left, and a bus waited to transport them away to basic training.

The specialist in the AMEDD called me two weeks later to inform me that everything had been approved. All that was needed now was for me to formally take my commission as a captain in the Army. Coincidently, Louisiana's State Surgeon, Colonel Philip Marler, would be in town in two days, and it was their suggestion that I meet them for my oath of office at that time. And meet them I did—at the Officers' Club at Camp Beauregard in Pineville. Melissa, Stuart, Deanna, and I waited in the entryway as the staff went to get Col. Marler.

After we greeted and shook hands, he confessed to me, "I've never sworn in anyone in a bar before!"

With that introduction, I raised my right hand and, like so many Americans before me, swore to "support and defend the Constitution of the United States against all enemies, foreign and domestic..." I was no longer a spectator.

Four

Patients In Green

⟨⟨⟩⟩

As we were about to leave the Officers' Club, the recruitment specialist advised me that in the next week or two, I would be contacted by the personnel officer from my assigned unit. When I had floated the idea of joining the military to my Dad, he had suggested that they would probably have me "in a clinic somewhere doing physicals." That really didn't sound too bad to me, as it wasn't too terribly different from what I was already doing in my residency continuity clinic. This was not to be the case.

As she flipped through my paperwork, she uttered this: "Wow. Field Surgeon in the Brigade. You're gonna be with some 'hooah' guys, sir." I reacted approvingly, but honestly didn't know how to react. I just knew that it did not sound like "in a clinic somewhere doing physicals." A week later, I got the call.

I had been assigned as the Battalion Surgeon for the 1st Battalion (1st Bn), 156th Armor Regiment. The

Regiment's impressive history dates back to 1769, and it had since been involved in nearly every conflict, beginning with the American Revolution. I would be the field physician to its several hundred soldiers — soldiers who drive tanks. At the time, 1st Bn was the principal armor component of Louisiana's 256th Brigade Combat Team (BCT) and was a fighting unit that was distinguished by the intimidating M1A1 Abrams main battle tank. I was told to report for my first drill at 7:00am in Shreveport and to link up with the Headquarters and Headquarters Company formation that would be assembled outside the armory. I was admittedly quite nervous about this.

As a physician, I had been directly commissioned into the Army because of my educational background — not like my friend Stuart, who had *earned* his commission after the rigor of Officer Candidate School. For all intents and purposes, I felt like a civilian who would be borrowing a soldier's uniform. I had learned in my welcome-to-the-1st Bn phone call that the entire 256th Brigade was busy preparing for a rotation at the Army's National Training Center (NTC) in Fort Irwin, California that summer — mere months away. Rather than attend the medical officer basic course in San Antonio, where I would be trained in military customs, I would be traveling with the unit to NTC. I did my best on that first drill morning to ensure that my pressed battle dress uniform was donned appropriately: every hole had the proper button, the black boots were polished, and my patrol cap was positioned right. The day before, I had gotten a haircut — a bit closer than I would normally. I hoped that I would not be doing push-ups in front of the formation, for appearance issues, at least!

Thankfully, I was able to find the armory with ease and navigated to the medic office prior to formation. I would be supervising a platoon of field medics of varying backgrounds. Some seemed barely 20 and fresh out of the Advanced Individual Training required to become an Army medic. The older guys nearly all worked healthcare jobs in the civilian world; many were EMTs or paramedics. I quickly befriended the medical supply sergeant who, recognizing my newness to the military experience, oriented me to the facility, the medics, and the battalion staff. Needless to say, the pace of activity that weekend was mind-boggling. Everywhere I went throughout the armory, soldiers were scurrying around with to-do lists, barking out acronyms that I had never heard in my life. All was in preparation for the NTC rotation in July. What I had already learned was that the NTC experience was a distinct privilege for a National Guard unit, one for which they had been preparing for over a year.

The Army's National Training Center rests in the Mojave Desert of southern California, situated halfway between Los Angeles and Las Vegas. It is every bit as harsh as it sounds. Surrounded by desert mountains, the NTC environment bakes in sunshine that sends July's average daily temperatures to over 100 degrees. Its rocky terrain crawls with rattlesnakes and Gila monsters, and serves as the most realistic simulation of desert combat the military can offer.

An active duty unit stationed at Fort Irwin provides the Opposition Force—or OPFOR—that embodies the enemy combat element. All vehicles, weapons, and personnel at NTC are equipped with the Multiple Integrated Laser Engagement System (MILES) that simulates hostile exchange and casualties. Really, the only things missing are the bullets. At the time of our rotation, the Brigade was involved in a mock combat operation against an OPFOR known as the "People's Democratic Republic of Kraznovia." As the rotational unit, we would be defending the friendly "Republic of Mojavia" against the invading Kraznovian army. It would involve pre-Cold War era movements of large assets across wide spans of terrain. And there would be casualties: intentionally simulated and accidentally real. As the weeks ticked down to my little trip to the sandbox, I became ever increasingly aware of my professional mortality: this would be the first time I would be on my own as a doctor. No upper level. No faculty. Just me and the reptiles.

As my family drove away after dropping me off at the armory in Shreveport, I found myself actually choking back emotion. This three-week jaunt to California would be the longest I had ever been away from home. Anyone entering the armory that night would have been convinced that we were going to war. Army green duffle bags were stacked everywhere. Haircuts were all screamingly close; most of the guys were nearly bald. Everyday glasses had been replaced by the combat-style black plastic frames with a rubber strap.

My auspicious indoctrination into military medicine would occur before we even left the armory. A young enlisted soldier eased into the medic office, followed by an imposing older gentleman. The soldier introduced himself, and sheepishly explained he had just been prescribed an antibiotic by his civilian doctor for a venereal infection. As he had perused the paragraphs of side effects, he fixated on, "Avoid exposure to the sun as burns may occur more easily," and subsequently believed that he should be excused from going to NTC. So did the guy behind him, who I soon learned was his father—a sergeant major from another unit. It could have been concluded by any observer in that room, Dad did not concur with my recommendations: that since his son was African-American, his darker skin tone markedly reduced this sunburn risk and moreover, he would have very little skin even exposed due to the required uniform.

Until then, I had never been yelled at by a family member—much less threatened with a lawsuit! Thankfully, at that low point, one of the medics had retrieved the battalion personnel officer to help extinguish the situation. After a counter threat of a Uniform Code of Military Justice referral for insubordination, the father backed down, and I wondered *what* I had gotten myself into! I crept off to a dark conference room within the armory, contorted myself into a vinyl armchair, and tried to get some sleep. In a few short hours, we would be on our way.

As we exited the plane in Victorville, California, I instantly recalled something my friend Stuart had observed from a prior rotation at NTC: "It just smells funky out there!" I don't know if it was due to lack of flowering vegetation or the oppressive heat or both, but he was right. And, of course, it was hot—like stepping off a plane into a hairdryer. Weeks before we had left home, we had been advised to start drinking water and perform light exercise in the heat to begin the acclimatization process. The risk of heat injury would be real and immediate.

As we stood in formation for the bus ride to Fort Irwin, I observed that no one was visibly sweating—despite the fact that it was already 98 degrees at 11:30 in the morning. Unlike our damp Louisiana climate, the desert had no humidity. While we were pouring sweat under the uniform, everything exposed was dry, as the water evaporated from the skin surface almost immediately. And therein lays the danger of dehydration in an arid environment: the persistent negative pressure that insidiously pulls water out of the body. By the time thirst begins, the fluid deficit is already significant. If the water is not replaced, and the body not cooled, the results can be disastrous. For that reason—among others—there would be a strict uniform policy that no sleeves would be rolled up. Water consumption would be mandated and monitored by the senior enlisted.

We boarded a convoy of buses and headed west toward Fort Irwin. We drove forever, in a trip that seemed as if we were leaving nowhere and going nowhere. Everything around was burnt and brown, all the way to the mountains that skirted the area. Finally the "Fort Irwin National Training Center" sign popped up on the horizon amid the sand and rocks. We were there.

The first several days would be spent in the "RUBA"—Rotational Unit Bivouac Area—where we would stage and prepare for battle. There was no king-size non-smoking with Jacuzzi here. It was a cot, on gravel, under a metal roof. I had brought my issue sleeping bag half-heartedly, thinking there was probably no conceivable way I needed an insulated sleeping bag in the desert in early July. I draped the bag over my cot and flopped over it in my shorts and t-shirt. At 12:30am, I woke—shivering! In just a few short hours, I had realized two facts of life that I had always spurned:

1. Desert heat is a dry heat

2. Deserts get really cold at night.

Every morning at 4:00am, I awoke to a succinct, "Alright, gentlemen," from Staff Sergeant Scott Caudle, the medic platoon sergeant. We donned the uniform and immediately ambled to the chow line for breakfast. I had never really been a voracious breakfast eater; it just took me a few hours awake to warm to the thought of food. But eggs, grits, bacon, sausage, French toast, and hash browns were just a bit more than I could negotiate in the middle of the night. It would not take me long to miss this Amish dairy farmer breakfast.

By our second day in the RUBA, the heat was already exerting its presence. Soldiers, at the firm behest of their first sergeants, were consuming up to a quart of water an hour. When over ten soldiers in the motor pool presented to our medical clinic within the same hour, complaining of nausea and vomiting, the command radar was raised. It did not take long to elucidate the source, as all of them complained that the water they drew from the "water buffalo" tank "tasted like chlorine." Indeed, chlorine *was* routinely utilized in the field to purify potable water, but when a quick analysis was performed on the buffalo-in-question, the levels were found to be ten times the recommended amount. In the end, it was chalked up to a simple measurement mistake by the NCO in charge of the water. He was reassigned.

With the battle plan established, we loaded our equipment onto our various tracked vehicles and headed for the "Box," where all the action would take place. While most of the line medics would operate out of the M113 personnel carrier, I was assigned to the larger M577—known as the "high-top shoe" for its suggesting profile. Inside were all of the necessary medical supplies to treat the real as well as the virtual casualty: intravenous fluids, surgical equipment, and a miniature pharmacy. Upon finding our ordered location somewhere in the desert, the rear ramp on the 577 dropped, and the Battalion Aid Station (BAS) was open for business. A collapsible shelter was attached off of the rear, where we were able to set up two patient litters on racks to serve as treatment beds. On the "walls" of the shelter were fastened pouches of fast-access items like fluids, tourniquets, dressings—even laryngoscopes (God forbid that would be needed!) Army doctrine provided that casualties would be evacuated at the point of injury by our line medics and then transported to the BAS for triage. Our location needed to provide conceal-ment as well as an efficient entry and exit point for our M113s. I would learn why the next day.

The first battle against the OPFOR was set to begin around sunrise. Our first mission would consist of a defense against a held position. The OPFOR would engage and attempt to penetrate our defensive perimeter. As always, our specific mission would be to provide medical support to the line companies, relocating as needed to support a mobile front. As the sun eased over the red mountains, distant cracks of simulated weapons fire resounded. And the M113s arrived. Most were filled to capacity with virtual casualties: soldiers adorned with tags that indicated the extent of their particular injuries. Some had minor flesh wounds. Others were already dead. Our medics off-loaded each casualty in the vicinity of the M577 and were directed to designated areas of priority. Those with the concurrence of high severity *and* hope of recovery were denoted the highest status. The guys with the minor scratches as well as the ones who were already dead—or nearly so—were blessed with a nap in the shade.

In the end, we achieved a decent result for the first battle. The dreaded "Died of Wounds" category was sufficiently low, as we were able to activate appropriate resuscitative care at our level and then arrange swift evacuation to higher echelons of capa-bility in the rear. After all of the day's action, I was dying for a good night's sleep on my cot in the back of our 2 ½ ton truck.

By 8:30pm, it was dark, and I had retired to the truck, gazing at the stars through my night vision goggles (NVGs). In the remote darkness of the desert, the constellations were Carl Sagan-brilliant through the NVGs. Meteorites that would have otherwise been invisible zipped through the atmosphere, and a broad gleam over the eastern horizon reminded me how close Las Vegas really was. It was then that I heard the pressured tapping on the rail of the truck.

"Doc! Doc! Somebody's been hurt."

I was up, dressed, and out of the truck in seconds. As I was running to the waiting M113, two of my medics informed me that one of our soldiers had been electrocuted while repairing some communications equipment roughly a mile away. They did not know any other details. We rumbled across the desert blackness in combat lights-out conditions, using only NVGs to guide us. Five minutes into our run, I was standing in the top hatch of the 113, guiding the driver, when I heard the most apocalyptic noise about 50 yards away. It was a combination of a diesel-powered banshee fused with a thunderstorm—like a jet roaring toward us on the ground. The vibration shot right up from the ground into our steel plating. I spun around to see the angular silhouette of an Abrams tank bounding over the sand dune to our left. It was obviously one of ours, trying to ascertain if we were friend or foe. It slammed to a halt and stared, breathing.

What I had just learned was that the Abrams *is* powered by a turbine engine—just like a jet. I also learned that in the quiet dark, there are few things on this earth more intimidating than 70 tons of wrath tumbling straight at you with its 120mm cannon trained on your face. Whoa. Enemies beware.

To my delight, we were able to quickly identify ourselves to the tank and proceeded to the location of our wounded comrade. Worst-case electrocution scenarios were spinning through my head. Third degree burns and cardiac arrest were both possibilities with severe electrocution, and I was hoping that I would be prepared for whatever we would find. Inside the tent, we thankfully found a conscious soldier with no visible injury. As he had been repairing an operational radio, an exposed wire had popped his finger—enough to where it rattled him and every other soldier in the tent. I listened to his heart and lungs, examined his hand, and reassured him that there was no latent danger. He was relieved—and so was the doctor!

I would joke with my civilian medical colleagues after I returned from California that the real-world problems out there were a Yogi Berra-esque 90% orthopedic and another 90% dermatologic. Sizzling heat and heavy metal objects combined to yield all permutations of rashes, bumps, sprains, and strains— along with the occasional heat exhaustion. My medics became proficient in starting IV fluids while knowing which tube of antifungal cream to recommend from the medicine case. Guys would actually come by *wanting* an elective IV, just to "perk themselves up" in the oven-like heat.

It was easy to identify the IVs started by the more junior medics by the streams of dried blood extending down the arm of the victim. After expending all of their technical energies placing the needle in the vein, they would often forget to keep pressure on the arm while hooking up the fluids. The result was brutally obvious!

I was impressed that nearly every soldier we treated, in spite of the infirmity, seemed actually *glad* to be in that desert. More than the jock itch or the sprained knee, they were focused on the mission to get back with their guys and beat the OPFOR. In my civilian training, I had grown accustomed to the physical ailment directing the patient's focus—and understandably so. When injuries or illnesses manifest in someone's life, their mental and physical energies are naturally directed inward in attempt to overcome whatever infirmity they are facing. Often however, the unfortunate result is that their entire existence becomes defined by *it*.

And while certainly these soldiers weren't dealing with mammoth issues like prostate cancer or Alzheimer's disease, I was still moved at the consistency of their mission-first mentality. A few lines from the U.S. Army Soldier's Creed, that I would later learn, left me with clear images of the guys I had cared for at NTC:

"I will always place the mission first.

I will never accept defeat.

I will never quit.

I will never leave a fallen comrade."

After nearly three weeks in the desert, I said goodbye to my medics and flew out early to Kansas

City, where the American Academy of Family Physicians was hosting its annual conference for residents and medical students. Our program had been invited to deliver a presentation delineating the differences between our specialty, internal medicine, and pediatrics. I was indeed glad that our commander had allowed me to leave a bit early, as I had worked on the presentation for months. After all of the sweltering heat, weekly showers, and Meals-Ready-to-Eat, walking into a hotel in Kansas City was akin to checking into Buckingham Palace to me. I was immediately mindful—and remain so—of the day-to-day luxuries we have as Americans. I have never forgotten that feeling or lost my appreciation for every day's blessings.

The process for licensure of physicians in the U.S. is a multi-staged process. As is the case for attorneys, CPAs, teachers, and other professionals, a certification exam is required in addition to the educational degree. In medicine, this is a three-part test known as the United States Medical Licensing Exam (USMLE). The first two parts are typically completed in medical school, while the third is attempted during internship, to examine one's ability to practice unsupervised medicine. Anxious to get it completed so that I could begin moonlighting, I had scheduled Step 3 for September 11 in Baton Rouge.

The morning of the test, I had left over an hour early to allow myself time to navigate the rush-hour traffic. I arrived at the testing center just before 8:00, switched off the "best of the 80s and today" station that I had been listening to, and went inside to check in for the test.

The testing center for these types of tests is essentially a hermetically sealed vault where the very air has audio and video surveillance. Instead of taking the allowed breaks between sections, I felt energized and plowed ahead with the test, finishing in about four hours. When I walked out of the testing room into the administrative office, I thought it odd that the employees were all so overtly just watching television with nothing to do. As one of them took my checkout papers, she explained to me that, "Somebody flew two airplanes into the World Trade Center."

Right. No way. I stood there in complete disbelief as I listened to the CNN reporter detailing a terrorist attack on New York, as well as another on the Pentagon. Like all Americans on that fateful day, I fell into a fog of surreal disbelief, not wanting to believe that such raw evil actually existed in the world. The images of those collapsing towers are seared into the brains of all Americans old enough to remember that day. The fire. The smoke. The loss of life. It was the day that life changed for us all. I could've never imagined exactly how much.

Five

A TV Show No More

In the weeks following 9/11, I, like so many other Americans, made every attempt to contrive some return to normalcy. Thankfully, the mighty demands of residency made this a less formidable task than for most, and within weeks I had gotten word of my passage of USMLE Step 3. The state license and Drug Enforcement Agency number soon followed. Mark Schneider had navigated these piles of paperwork and fees a couple of months earlier, and had already begun moonlighting in area emergency rooms. I devoured his stories of patients he had treated and heroic procedures he had performed. But despite my level of training and my brief stay in the desert, I was admittedly a little intimidated at the thought of being completely alone as a doctor at some little hospital two hours from the boonies. Yet as is often declared in medicine, "The risks outweighed the benefits." The experience would be a singular competence —

and confidence—builder, and the income for one weekend approached what we made in an entire month as residents. I scheduled my first ER shift.

Naturally, the contract companies that staff most emergency departments schedule physicians at facilities that are commensurate with their experience. Since I was a relative novice to autonomous emergency room work, I was scheduled at a location where the overall volume was low, as was the chance of a major trauma presentation. Jackson Parish Hospital in Jonesboro, Louisiana served as my indoctrination site. Jonesboro is a tiny town curled into the deep piney woods of north Louisiana, just above the land of Huey P. Long. The shift would start at 6:00pm on Friday night and go all the way until 6:00am Monday morning—60 total hours. Of course, the work demand would be sporadic, and I was told most of the time I would either be sleeping or watching TV. I was dearly hoping that this wasn't simply *recruiterese* on the part of the scheduler.

I arrived about 20 minutes early to Jonesboro, evading the ubiquitous logging trucks that might have slowed me down on the winding highway north. As I crept in the ambulance entrance to the ER, I became consumed with my insecurities. I think if there had been something critical in one of the exam rooms when I arrived, the staff would have found me curled in a fetal position somewhere. As it was, the ER was empty, and I was met by a wonderful nurse named Bonita Caskey, who toured me through the department and to my call room. The room was spacious; it needed to be, for the entire medical reference library

I had brought with me! And so 6:00pm arrived, and I bunkered myself in the call room, waiting for the inevitable phone call from the night nurse.

My plan would be to get a preliminary report from the nurse as to what the presenting patient was complaining of. As soon as I hung up the phone, I would zip through any pertinent information in those books to refresh my memory on what to watch out for and what the key treatment points were. Nearly all of what I saw that weekend were conditions that I had seen before. I just hadn't treated them alone in the woods.

The first, shall we say, unique encounter occurred early Saturday afternoon. Bonita was back on shift and called to tell me that there was a man who had just arrived with a "splinter in his butt." (I didn't bother checking the reference books for that one.) The 40-something guy explained to me that he had been sitting on a wooden park bench with his pet English bulldog when the dog playfully lunged at a sausage snack that was hanging from his mouth. In an effort to avoid the snap of his dog, he slid across the bench, and subsequently took on a sizeable shard of it in his right buttock. Fortunately, between his recollection of the story and my explanation of how I would extract the splinter, we built a pretty good rapport. With not much pressure, I could feel what seemed like a three to four inch-long object that had broken off deep in the skin and extended into the muscle. As I injected a local anesthetic to the puncture site, he expressed to me something I will never forget:

"Doc, I'll bet you've never dug a splinter this big out of a man's ____!"

He was right. Amid the chuckles, I incised into the wound to widen it so that I could dissect down to the splinter. Within a half inch of exploration, the dark brown end of the splinter became visible. I clamped down on it with a straight hemostat and began pulling. The plank that came forth was easily four inches long—and hardly could be considered a *splinter!*

The anecdotes are unfortunately not all so favorable in their remembrance. The next morning, the phone rang earlier than it had on Saturday, and this time it was no splinter. The ambulance service was bringing in a young woman who had apparently suffered a spontaneous miscarriage. What they didn't yet know was how far along she had been at the time. As the paramedics whisked her into the exam room, I couldn't help but notice the strained look on her face as she made every attempt to restrain the emotional explosion she was experiencing.

Through the tears, she explained that she had awakened about 30 minutes before with severe abdominal cramping and bleeding. Within minutes, EMS had arrived, and her 15-week pregnancy had unfortunately terminated. After they had ensured that she wasn't bleeding, the paramedics had wisely not taken any further interventions. What we discovered was a perfectly formed fetus—about six inches long, still tethered by the tiny umbilical cord. After I had assisted her in completing the delivery, I tried in my awkward male way to console her. I didn't offer any platitudes or give any speeches. Sometimes an "I am so sorry for your loss," and a hand on the shoulder, are the very best we can give.

In between these standout points of recollection, I saw any number of lacerations, intoxications, and cases of chest pain, and sometimes—in the company of law enforcement—I encountered all three in the same patient. I had always liked repairing lacerations, dating back to my first lesson in suturing by Dr. LaRavia (using a pig's foot as a patient!). In the emergency room, I quickly became adroit at putting them in *live* tissue and on patients with varying levels of cooperation. And out in the country, any number of foreign objects might find their way gouged into flesh somewhere it was not intended to be: fishhooks, gravel, and steel shot were all commonly extracted—with the occasional splinter.

One Sunday night in Jonesboro, I had just sat down, exhausted, in front of the TV, fully ready to relax until 6:00 the next morning. The phone rang with an early warning: ambulance bringing in a 52-year-old man with chest pain, and "they think it's for real." As common as chest pain is as a presenting symptom to the emergency department, it is not nearly as common that heart attacks are actually captured in progress. As soon as I saw this guy wheel up the ramp, however, I knew the paramedics were right. He was sick.

Even after three nitroglycerin and an injection of morphine, he was still dripping sweat down his face and looked uncomfortable. As he related the nature of his pain to me, the nurses were hooking up the

EKG electrodes to his chest. What I saw spit out of the EKG printer stopped me in mid-sentence across the room: the most profound heart injury pattern I had ever seen on a patient. I made no attempt to whitewash the situation to him or his family, and we immediately began working on his transfer to a higher acuity hospital with cardiology support. An aggressive medicine cocktail was poured into his IV, and thankfully his level of pain began to abate. The accepting cardiologist with whom I spoke in Monroe did not hesitate for an instant in requesting that we bundle him up, put a bow on him, and get him on the road. He would be going to the heart catheterization lab that night.

By 3:30am, I was in a well-deserved R.E.M. sleep coma when the phone rang again. This time, it was the cardiologist in Monroe. My own heart stopped. He was simply calling to let me know that the gentleman we sent had gone to the cath lab, had a stent placed in the offending blockage, and was doing well. Wonderful. I never went back to sleep— irrespective of the coma.

There were few feelings of occupational satisfaction as profound as the one that kicked in at 6:00am those Monday mornings. It was an endorphin surge somewhat akin to completing a marathon or climbing Mt. Everest [and I have done neither!] With my victory cup of coffee in hand, I would hit the road in the dark and head home—so that I could be at work in two hours. I was finally able to relate some war stories of my own in the doctors' lounge, doing my darnedest to quell any old-man's-fishing-tale embellishment. Yet regardless of any personal edification, my patients—both military and civilian—benefited from a more seasoned, confident doctor. Residency training, emergency medicine work, and military experience were each mutually beneficial components to my maturation as a physician, and by the end of my residency, I knew I would be just that much more prepared for independent decision making.

It was also during this time that Melissa and I welcomed another little Hunterette into the world. Avery Rae opened her big, soon-to-be-brown eyes on December 27, 2002. Grayson got her wish with a baby sister, and the Hunter sorority house was complete.

By the end of 2002, residency was already drawing to its final stages. The experiences were as rich and diverse as I had hoped they would be. I had been selected as one of the chief residents and carried out its dubious honor as the Chief Schedule Maker and subsequent Chief Complaint Taker. My technical and clinical judgment skills were compounding themselves, and I was accumulating a large panel of patients in my continuity clinic, with whom I developed some great relationships. I continued the ER work, gradually stepping up the acuity level at busier facilities. I even briefly entertained the thought of full-time emergency medicine with its lure of flexible scheduling and no call. But in the end, I knew God had called me to be a family doc, and I could not carry that out to its fullest in the ER.

During that point of decision, I ran into Dr. Joan Brunson at the hospital. Joan had graduated residency two years ahead of me and had joined a prestigious family medicine group across the street. She inquired about my plans for that fall. When I told her of my lean toward emergency medicine, she expressed her regret and countered with a pitch:

"We're happy with four doctors now, but we'd like you to be our fifth. If you don't come, we're just gonna stay at four."

Wow. I was honored even to be considered by the partners at the Brian Clinic and thanked her for their consideration. The Brian Clinic was a deeply established group of family docs, with roots going back a half-century. Two of the very finest senior residents I had known at the LSU program were now there, and the prospect of working there was powerfully tempting. I told Joan that I would think on it seriously.

At the beginning of my continuity clinic the following week, Myranda Brossette, my nurse at the residency, handed me a phone message from a Mr. John Stigall at the hospital. At the time, John was the Vice President at Rapides Regional who directed physician recruitment, and I was reasonably confident in the nature of his call. Across the country, it is fairly standard for physicians to be recruited to a practice by a partnering hospital. The hospital basically funds the startup costs in return for a specified term of full-time practice in the area. John was calling at the request of the Brian Clinic's managing partner, Dr. Greg Brian. It was a formal request to dinner, where an offer would be presented. By then, Melissa and I were beginning to feel that central Louisiana was home for us. I had explored positions in other areas, but after all the years of college and residency, we realized we were already in the place where God wanted us. I called John Stigall back, and we agreed to a dinner the following week.

As we walked into the Bistro on the Bayou, we were ushered back to the meeting room where the four partners were already seated around a large table. As soon as the food orders were placed, Greg began an introduction to the history of the Brian Clinic: the story of its founding partners, those who came along later, and the most recent additions. His assurances were as solid and straightforward as his reputation in the local medical community: "We know how to run a business; we've been doing it for a long time. All you need to bring is your white coat and a stethoscope."

This held particular attraction to me, as I had been utterly paralyzed at the thought of purchasing equipment and leasing office space on my own. After all, a business school graduate I was not. Greg also confirmed the obvious benefit of working in a partnership as a family doctor—a division of labor in a job with considerable demands. And he then offered a caveat that would prove prophetic: "If you should ever get deployed with the military, we will be here to take care of your patients." The deal was signed two weeks later.

By early 2003, American military action in Iraq seemed imminent, and with it began furtive rumors about the possibility of reservist deployments. The opinions were mixed. Many ex-military people with whom I spoke chalked it all up to nothing but a bunch of saber rattling, while the Gulf War vets who had just finished shaking Kuwaiti sand out of their boots were less optimistic. They had been down this same road before in 1991 and were keenly sensitized to the type of rhetoric that precluded an overseas invitation. Frankly, the slightest contemplation of flying into a war zone was unthinkable to me. The daily threat of death and the extended separation from my little family were two things I could not bear the thought of. Grayson had grown into a precious little pre-schooler, and Avery was, in my mind, still a baby. In many ways, I still felt like that same goofy civilian-in-uniform on the first day of drill back in Shreveport.

On March 20, the war began, as did my march toward inevitability.

By April, with the invasion of Iraq in full swing, I was notified by my unit personnel officer, Captain Randy Green, that rather than accompany the Battalion to Fort Polk for that summer's annual training exercise, I had finally gotten a slot at the Medical Officer's Basic Course (OBC) conducted at Fort Sam Houston, Texas. Rather than the nine grueling weeks of basic training endured by army enlistees, this was a compact two-week course designed for medical officers in the reserve component. It is sometimes affectionately termed "Salute and Shoot" for obvious reasons: it is the formal introduction to the basics of military customs and operations. From how to shine your boots to how to fire the

M9 pistol, it is the "Soldiering for Dummies" course for all of us wannabees. It includes lectures on Army structure and doctrine of medical operations—even a brief field training exercise at the nearby Camp Bullis (where the tents are air-conditioned).

I actually looked forward to the OBC, for no more reason than to learn what I had been doing or wearing incorrectly for the past two years. The assembly auditorium for the opening brief was huge, and it needed to be. Hundreds of people had already taken their seats. More were trickling in. Captain James Hayes was the course director and began the opening remarks with a message of gratitude for agreeing to serve the country at such a pivotal time in history. He asked,

"How many of you made the decision to join the Army after September 11?"

More than a fourth of the room stood, and applause resounded—rightfully so. I was in awe of each of them. Unlike my own, their commitment to the United States military was inked with complete awareness of *likely* implications. I gazed at them as I clapped away and honestly wondered if I would have had the courage to do the same. Each was an accomplished civilian medical professional in their own right. And each had said they were willing to leave home, job, and family for the defense of freedom. With that, Captain Hayes delved into the absolutely vital role of the Army Medical Department in the War on Terror, with global demands drawing American fighting strength into battle. He hearkened back to the day when the likelihood of reservist deployments overseas was slim.

"Today," he explained, "it's not a matter of *if* but *when*. You will all get your turn."

I felt a sinking flush pour over me as my feeble attempts at denial washed away. It looked like I would get a turn after all.

Six

Get A Job

───◈───

By the time I had successfully navigated Officer's Basic Course and returned home, the completion of residency was literally days away. And with it, the buildup to the start of my practice at the Brian Clinic. While my residency classmates contemplated the price of one EKG machine over another, or the amount of money to pay their employees, I ordered three new white coats and polished my stethoscope. The hospital took a few photos and was already prepping the advertising blitz that would preclude my August 4th start date. And thankfully, with my decision to stay in Alexandria, many of the patients I had acquired in residency were already requesting the transfer of their records.

Patients weren't the only acquisition from residency that I would assume, however. I needed a nurse. Myranda Brossette had been my nurse at LSU long enough that I already felt personal ownership of her in my continuity clinic. She was not far out of nursing school at the time, but had a work ethic and communication skills that were qualities of a nurse years her senior. As my third year of residency training had progressed, my patient volume had increased dramatically, and with it, the need for reliable efficiency in the clinic. Whether on the phone—which she operated like a Stradivarius—or face-to-face with a patient, she was unwaveringly polite and displayed great clinical judgment. The patients loved her. It was largely because of her influence that my continuity experience achieved its level of success. Not surprisingly, I decided to not give her up.

Thankfully, Myranda agreed to leave an outstanding job at LSU to come down the street and be the sole nurse to a rookie doctor. Her recognizable face and voice made my patients' transition to a new doctor's office that much more comfortable. And so, on August 4th, I donned the starchy new white coat—embroidered with the succinct "Jonathan D. Hunter, MD"—and headed off for my first 9:30 appointment.

The patient who filled that slot was a gentleman I had been treating at LSU for over a year. There, he had previously been cared for by a faculty physician who had relocated, and the faculty doctor had suggested his assignment to me prior to his departure. The patient was the owner of a local transportation company and was known to personify many of the stereotypes of a chief executive: terse, deliberate, loud, and exacting. Yet the faculty member had regarded this man as one of his favorite patients. My very first encounter took place in my second year. After having been briefed on the appropriate royal protocol by my faculty friend, I lifted his chart from the door, took a deep breath, and scooted in the room. He darted to his feet and grabbed my hand with an iron clasp. I reciprocated. With his face no more than six inches from my own, staring straight through my eye sockets drill sergeant-style, he introduced himself. We sat. Over the next two minutes, he asked all the questions:

"Where are you from?"

"Where did you go to college?"

"Where did you go to medical school?"

"How are you liking residency?"

"What are your plans after residency?"

With the same gusto with which he stood when I entered the room, he jumped up again, "Well, I like what I see. When do you want to see me back?"

It was the only occasion I have ever been interviewed *by* a patient, and I had fortunately passed. Our doctor-patient relationship flourished in the months afterward, and I came to know him also as a friend. At one point, when I had expressed my contemplation of full-time emergency medicine in south Louisiana, he didn't express disappointment at the prospect of losing his doctor. He simply responded, "That's okay. I'll get a hotel room down there for a day."

So, it was only fitting that the ceremonial opening pitch would be his at 9:30 on August 4th. He was already standing in the room when I entered. He hugged me, told me he was proud of me, and commented that he liked my "new digs." With that, my real job began.

Over the next several weeks, along with the surge of former LSU patients, new patients began trickling in as well. Fostered by a few radio and newspaper plugs, my schedule began to show more names than blank slots. Yet with word of mouth being one of the most effective advertising devices, satisfied customers bred even more of the same. And while the services I provided for my patients were largely the same as they had been in residency, private practice had a completely different feel. For the first time, they truly belonged to *me*. I was their doctor. They were my patients. No faculty. No program. And with that economy of understanding, came a level of responsibility that I had never known previously.

As family physicians, we are trained to evaluate patients holistically by means of a psychosocial approach. It is not enough to elicit a thorough history, perform a focused physical exam, and deduce the correct diagnosis. Modern family doctors are taught to do all of this while still allowing for the possible influence of psychological and interpersonal factors. Most of us are drawn to family medicine *because* of this broadened consideration. We consequently often find ourselves doing much more than making diagnoses and writing prescriptions; we are sometimes the pastor, counselor, and friend as well. And I have found that in many cases, the difference between a good doctor and a dynamic doctor is defined by how well those "secondary" roles are managed.

The patients who were drawn to my fledgling practice were totally diverse. From small children to children who had just gotten too cool for the cartooned walls of the pediatrician's office, I began accumulating a fair number of youngsters. Most of their parents loved the concept of everyone going to the same physician, and they typically came along for the ride. Ages extended from there all the way to senior adults, many of whom possessed profound medical needs. Walking into each exam room meant walking into a completely unique life experience — some short, and some quite long. I found myself doing all of the talking to a 12-year-old in one room, and doing all the listening with a wise nonagenarian in the next.

Because of Alexandria's regional healthcare identity in central Louisiana, and in no small measure due to my work in area emergency departments, people within an hour's radius began calling for appointments. From "Northerners" in the Winnfield area, all the way southeast to the Cajuns of Avoyelles Parish, folks gladly made the pilgrimage to Alexandria. I would have never imagined that people would be willing to drive an hour to go to the doctor, but they did. Before too long, I found myself having less and less time to throw darts at the board in my office. Patients begat more patients, and I had become busy.

By the spring of 2004, the boiling insurgency in Fallujah had resulted in the assassination and public parading of four American contract workers through its streets. With the free world given even more insight into the bottomless hatred faced in this war, Louisiana's

256 Brigade was prepared for action. 1st Battalion was alerted for deployment in March, and with it, so was I. Whereas in the earlier stages of contemplation, I had been absolutely unable to process the thought of deploying to Iraq, I now had been ruminating on the possibility for months—and so had Melissa. By the time the email notices from the mobilization officer trickled in, we were not shocked. Melissa had delved into electronic message boards posted by wives of deployed soldiers and had drawn from the encouragement of some very supportive friends—one of whom was Stuart West's wife, Deanna. Stuart would, after all, be there with me.

By now there are few remaining superlatives left to properly describe the sacrifices made by the families of deployed service members. While the battles are being fought thousands of miles away, *they* are the ones left behind to do the homework, pay the bills, and give the baths—day after day, often with little assistance. And while grinding through the monotony and loneliness of these routines, a shroud of stress grays everything. Uncertainty and fear are constant and can't simply be prayed away. Only God's daily provision can provide the strength to endure. Melissa had been blessed by the testimonies of countless wives testifying to this truth, and she was ready.

On September 8, 2004, after just over a year in practice, I received an email with the following request:

*"...Pursuant to Presidential Executive Order...
You are ordered to active duty...in Support of
Operation Iraqi Freedom."*

That moment was not cinematic. I didn't begin
moaning despondently. I didn't curl into a corner and
start sucking my thumb. I have to admit that a significant part of me was relieved—relieved to finally
be past the speculation. And I am pretty sure that
Melissa felt the same way. The way I had come to
view it all was simple: I was a soldier. Soldiers fight
wars. Others had gone before me, and this was my
turn to go. God had brought me to this place in His
providential wisdom [Romans 8:28], and He would
bear my family and me through this great challenge
through the power of His Spirit.

I was oddly reminded of a lecture by my physics
professor at Louisiana College, Dr. Donald Sprowl. In
an introduction to electromagnetics, he explained that
because of its relative newness to the world of scientific knowledge, it remained a field fraught with nearly
as many confusing complexities as basic answers.
By contrast, the older laws of Newtonian mechanics
were right because the depth of their truth rested in
the "beauty" of their simplicity. I found that to apply
in countless cases since. Salvation by grace through
faith was one. An invitation to Iraq was another.

Word of my impending departure zipped through
our community like lightning. Alexandria's local paper
devoted a feature article to my deployment, complete
with color photo, and the word was out. Prepared
by all of the media attention given throughout the

state to the mobilization of the Brigade, most of my patients reacted with little surprise to the news. There were many hugs, many reassurances, many promises of prayer for my family and me. Men, regardless of their ability to comply, offered to assist Melissa with anything at home: from cutting the lawn to changing light bulbs. Each day at work became an endless response to the same interrogatory:

"Dr. Hunter, did I hear that you're…[people often wouldn't know what to say here]?"

"Oh, my gosh. How are Melissa and the girls?"

"When are you leaving?"

"How long will you be gone?"

"What are you going to be doing over there?"

Patients, friends, hospital staff, and pharmaceutical reps all wanted to know the same details, but as the weeks ticked down, I have to admit that I had grown weary of the discussion. When I entered an exam room to see a patient, I longed for them to immediately launch into a dissertation about how the new pill I had prescribed at their last visit wasn't working. I wanted the pharmaceutical salespeople to greet me with their familiar handshake and start flipping the pages of their new promotional piece. It was not to be. They were all far more interested in another issue.

One notable example was a 40-something patient I had been treating for several months. Like most men of that age, trips to the doctor are categorized somewhere with mall shopping and insurance seminars. Yet because of some rather hefty medical issues, his visits to the Brian Clinic had been frequent. A week after the newspaper article had run, he was in my office for another follow-up. Before we delved into his symptoms and medicines, he dropped a heavy silver bracelet on the counter between us. He explained that his deceased father had served in Vietnam as an Army combat medic. His men had so revered him there that they all pitched in to buy him a steel link bracelet engraved with the word "DOC." After his father's death, it had obviously been a very special memento of his service.

"Until now, I had never had a doctor that I liked. Before you go, I want you to have it."

I really did not know what to say. There is no description for the kind of humility I was sensing, and to say, "oh no—I really couldn't take that," would have been a total insult. Instead, I thanked him for entrusting me with something so special, and I assured him that I would treasure it for the rest of my professional career. It was more than a gift. Amid all of the hugs and tearful eyes and admonitions to keep my head down, that bracelet was a static reminder of heartfelt, legitimate concern on the part of many. I was ashamed of my previous self-centeredness. People really did care—and not just because they were losing their doctor for a few months.

With no more than a handful of days remaining, Melissa and I were invited by my "inaugural patient" to his home for dinner. He and his wife had spared no expense—had even had a friend come to cater the event just for us. We relaxed on the outdoor deck that provided the blissful view of a sunset across the lake, and tried to discuss things other than the obvious.

When we finally sat at the table, in his typical commandeering, alpha male style, he immediately raised his glass for a toast. We all complied. In a toast unlike any I had ever witnessed, he closed his eyes and began,

"Dear Lord, I want to pray for the safety of my friend..."

The remainder was a tearful plea for the well-being of me and my family. It was moving. And I will certainly never forget it.

I took the last week off from work to savor a few last precious moments with Melissa and the girls. Melissa and I had elected to spend one of our very last weekends together watching the Fighting Tigers of LSU demolish the Bulldogs of the University of Georgia between the hedges at Sanford Stadium. We had the bright idea of getting "good" seats instead of those relegated to the visiting team. Mistake. On October 2, we were drowned in a sea of red and black woofing fans—and watched our Tigers *get* demolished, 45-16. I can say that Athens was beautiful, and we had a great weekend together in Atlanta—despite what was impending.

Melissa and I took care of one last piece of business in the week prior to my departure. She and the girls had recently driven to Natchez, Mississippi to have portraits made by a photographer there by the name of T.G. McCary. A viewing of the proofs was needed so the portrait selection could be made, and we had decided to go do that after we had gotten back from Georgia. When we entered the viewing room in his studio, I could see that this would be much more than simply flipping through some photos laid out on a table. The lights were dimmed, and the LCD projector came on—along with some soft music. The photos began, complete with the obligatory smooth fade. They were just perfect. I had never seen pictures of my wife and children that so accurately captured their beauty. But by the fourth picture, the combination of the portraits, the music, and current events overwhelmed my emotional capacity to handle it all. I lost it—became a total blubbering idiot, and didn't see one more picture. And I have never been one so inclined. I can only say that it is a good thing that Melissa held it together, or the pictures never would have been selected. Interestingly, McCary acted as if my reaction were expected; apparently the fathers always crumble first!

Seven

Go East, Young Man

—⁕—

Saturday, October 10, 2004. In my woodland green camouflage uniform, I posed with the girls in our front yard for some sendoff snapshots. Grayson was six and Avery was two. Interestingly, the girls smiled as if I were *returning* home instead of leaving. By the time we reached the airport, however, the pictures told a different story. One that breaks my heart to this day is a close-up of Avery holding my hand as I prepared to go through the security checkpoint. She held onto my hand with both of hers and just stared ahead—the grin from earlier that morning long gone. Again, there was no Hollywood moment. No sobbing. No despair. The strength that I had prayed for God to grant my family and me had welled within us all. Our goodbyes were all encouraging: reminders to be safe, call any time, and the obligatory, "I'll be home soon." I gave one final kiss to each of my girls, and a long embrace with Melissa. I clenched my fake smile and I turned to enter the security gate.

I have never jumped off a cliff or out of an airplane, but I can't imagine how my sentiments at that point would have differed much. Even now, years later, the ubiquitous news coverage of departing soldiers evokes an instant visceral reaction within me—as I'm sure it does in anyone whose has had that experience. Watching those hugs and kisses, the crying spouses and children, the turn to board the plane is a deep thing; there are hardly enough adjectives to cover it.

I would be traveling from Alexandria to Fort Bliss, Texas. At the time, Fort Bliss housed one of the Army's two Continental United States Replacement Centers (CRC), where individuals—not units—both military and civilian were readied and then sent to theaters of operation around the world. I would be navigating the CRC with four other physicians and one dentist from Louisiana—all also being deployed to support the Brigade. I was flying that day with Dr. John Miller, a lieutenant colonel and fellow LSU Family Medicine Residency Program graduate. I had known John for several years, and was delighted to encounter at least one familiar face as I sat down in the passenger waiting area. We had each discovered the news of our deployment at roughly the same time, and we had been in contact many times over the preceding weeks. John and I shared the same background, faced the same uncertainties, and had the same apprehensions about what lay ahead. Not to mention his diminutive stature and affable personality reminded me acutely of my father—I almost felt like Dad was going with me!

Fort Bliss is located in El Paso, right on the border with Ciudad Juarez, Mexico. It is a high desert plain environment—right out of a spaghetti Western. Viewing the sand and mountains from above was an appropriate appetizer for what was to come, but we were not headed to the set for *A Fistful of Dollars.* The folks checking in at the CRC were astonishingly diverse—far more so than I expected. For starters, the group was at least half civilian, and the civilians were a fascinating group of people. Many were ex-military headed to Iraq for treacherous contract security work. They were fairly easy to spot, as many of them maintained some part of their appearance that gave a nod to their previous lives: shaved heads, unit tattoos, a noticeable military bearing. However, most did contrast this with at least one feature that had been disallowed before. The long goatees were the most common. I can say unequivocally that they were all bad dudes, intimidating behind their black shades—even without semiautomatic arms. I would have been glad to have them protecting me over there! The remainder of the civilians was a smattering of service contractors and journalists. Most had similar goals regardless of background: the willingness to confront profound risk in exchange for a six-figure reward. As I eavesdropped on their conversations, most planned to pay off a mortgage, *get* a mortgage, or maybe start a business of their own. For those few, the road to the American dream would pass right through southwest Asia.

The military personnel converging on Fort Bliss that week were mostly medical. Like us, they were mobilized guardsmen and reservists heading over the Atlantic to fill individual, vital roles in direct support of combat operations. A few were senior officers and enlisted who had done this before in the early nineties, but most were new to the deployment experience. The physicians I met were all fascinating people in their own right, with a widely diverse array of specialties. Colonel Stephen Ulrich was a family physician who served as the State Surgeon for Ohio's Army National Guard. He was an incredibly inter- esting, gregarious guy—one of those who was never *not* engaged in a conversation with someone. He was a partner in the Perry County Family Practice, a single-specialty group exactly like my own. Perry County is a mostly rural region of Ohio, just south- east of where I had grown up. Until then, I had never heard of a family doc who would *fly his own helicopter* to attend patients in satellite clinics! He beamed me his contact information from his PDA so that we could keep in touch while we were both in Iraq, and he was off to his next "interview." The rest of the doctors were equally memorable: a father and son—both physicians, both deploying to Iraq. Another was a trauma surgeon from New Jersey who was an expert in the treatment of gunshot wounds, headed to a forward surgical team somewhere in the Sunni Triangle.

After the next four days at the CRC, I had earned an honorary doctorate in waiting-in-line studies. Hours upon hours were spent navigating through a seemingly endless list of stations spread throughout Fort Bliss. Monday was spent completing the extensive medical screening that asserted our physical readiness for an overseas deployment. I was one of the few fortunate individuals who did not have any immunization records through the Army. While the guys around me were getting anywhere from two to three shots, I was getting…11. Hepatitis, smallpox, anthrax, and all the rest of the third world's potential pathogens were addressed all the way down both arms. When I walked away from that station, I felt like I had been in a bar fight — and lost badly.

That night, I placed a call to Columbus, Ohio where my paternal grandmother had just been readmitted to the hospital. "Granny" had been declining for months due to worsening congestive heart failure—to the point that Dad and I had flown there weeks before my departure, ostensibly to say goodbye. When I had walked into her hospital room then, I knew that there was nothing ostensible about it. She drifted into alertness long enough for us all to have a good visit—and long enough for me to kiss her and tell her that I loved her before we left.

As I attempted a conversation with her in the CRC office at Fort Bliss, it was obvious that her time was indeed limited. This time, she was hardly lucid enough to respond to me. And once again, I found myself at the brink of an emotional meltdown—this time with an audience. Between leaving home and family and strapping on a pistol to fly into a war zone, the imminent loss of my grandmother was an added strain that I would have preferred to avoid. Life does not always revolve around our preferences. My Aunt Lila returned to the phone and asked if I would go ahead and write a eulogy for Granny before I left. I agreed with her that it would be needed soon. That was not an easy thing to compose there in that office, but I had enough time, and it came out as I wanted— remembering Granny for the love and strength that had shaped us all. I ended her eulogy with a line from my favorite old hymn, "It Is Well with My Soul." It was written by Horatio Spafford, a man who had endured Job-like personal loss in his life. He had first lost a son, then much of his personal fortune in the Chicago fire of 1871. Two years later, his wife and four daughters were on a ship bound for England when it collided with another vessel, killing many of the passengers—including all four of Spafford's daughters. A telegram sent to Mr. Spafford by his wife read only, "Saved alone." It is said that as he crossed the Atlantic, when his own ship had reached the location of the accident, he penned the words to the now timeless hymn. My favorite verse has always been the third, where he described the victory of salvation through Christ's crucifixion. I could think of no better way to end Granny's eulogy than with the last line, "Praise the Lord, praise the Lord, O my soul!"

Tuesday was the day appropriated for issuing all of the clothing and equipment required for deployment to Southwest Asia—four crammed duffle bags worth, along with the 9mm pistol that I would hopefully never require. The next day I *did* require it—on the qualification range, where we were required to hit a few knockdown targets a few meters away. With that, I was qualified to hit the side of a barn while inside it. After observing my performance and that of the doctors who fired with me, I was quite convinced of one fact of war: *if the doctors have been called upon to defend you, things are decidedly bad.*

Thursday, we were briefed on theater-specific readiness issues related to everything from Muslim social customs to improvised explosive devices (IEDs). I attempted to learn a few Arabic phrases—"Peace be with you," "hello," and "thank you" were a good start, but I hoped that I would never be in a position where my Arabic proficiency was a requisite. By Friday, the fast track process was complete. Our desert camouflage uniforms had returned from the seamstress, the duffel bags of equipment were packed, and our papers were validated. It was time to fly.

Contrary to what many believe, not all soldiers fly into war strapped inside a gargantuan C-130. As we left the massive holding room with the equally massive American flag, we walked out to a waiting civilian airliner. Our luggage had already been searched twice by bomb-sniffing canines and had been loaded on the plane. We were given a farewell salute and handshake on the tarmac by the CRC commander, and we were off to Maryland. From Baltimore, we zoomed across the Atlantic to Frankfurt, Germany. When we touched down there, it was approximately 1:30am. And despite the time, everyone was glad at the prospect of getting off the plane after eight hours of sitting—even with the in-flight movies. Upon exiting the jetway, a group from the United Service Organizations (USO) was waiting for us with handshakes, applause, and refreshments. Talk about love—at 1:30 in the morning! We were all amazed at that level of dedication and selflessness. After their coffee and cookies, we had about an hour to snag a cold water shave and check out the offerings in the shopette there in the terminal. Then it was time to re-board and continue east.

It was my first experience with a lengthy overseas flight, and I attempted to get some sleep here and there with all of the activity on the plane. Six more hours groaned by. Anyone who has ever flown has become conditioned to the "We have begun our initial descent" speech. Until that day, the tail end of that sentence had always been completed by a destination that inferred some degree of glad anticipation—some city in Ohio or Texas or Louisiana, where loved ones would be waiting. Kuwait City did not qualify accordingly. Even though it was still dark, I could make out the sheen of the infamous Persian Gulf. Kuwait City appeared massive. It could have easily been mistaken for Miami or Los Angeles, were it not for the spire of Liberation Tower gouging the night sky along with the scattered peaks of mosques throughout the skyline. It was obviously a modern, cosmopolitan city, but the Middle Eastern fingerprint was unmistakable. As I hopped off the last step onto the tarmac, the obligatory declaration to Toto about Kansas seemed irrepressible.

My first encounter with the gravity of our new surroundings took place as we filed to the shuttle buses that would transport us from the airport to

Camp Doha. The appearance of each bus was exactly like that of any commercial charter: plush seats, air conditioning, and television. But I had never seen curtains drawn over the windows of a Greyhound. They were clearly meant to hide the passengers from anyone who might be considering an attack on a target as "soft" as a bus. As we pulled out onto the highway, I peeked through the curtains just enough to see a Kuwaiti military Jeep fall in behind our bus—a Jeep with yellow flashers and a .50 caliber machine gunner standing in the back. The occasional Mercedes or BMW would pass us on the left—a reminder of the wealth of this oil-sodden little nation. They were all driven by men with the familiar checkered *ghutra* draped over their heads, and they all seemed to accelerate rather deliberately to get around the convoy of buses. With a 500-round-per-minute machine gun angled in my direction, I reasoned that I would make every effort to get out of there as well.

Camp Doha was formerly an industrial warehouse complex that had been converted to a U.S. Army base during the Gulf War. In addition to being an operational center for Central Command (CENTCOM), it had become a pivotal transit point for forces moving into and out of Iraq. We exited the buses, where the mountains of green duffle bags were being piled on the sidewalk, and I hoped the strategic strip of red tape I had placed on my bags would allow me to locate them before the end of the war. We were immediately ushered into a large conference room nearby, where we would get the mandatory series of briefings for all service members entering this theater. It was also the place where we would "swipe in," and I could not have been more anxious to do so. "Swiping in" was the term given to the swipe of the military ID card through the computer to document official entry into the theater of operations. It also started the 90-day clock for my fellow physicians and me. After my card had whisked through that reader, I knew that every second moved me that much closer to home.

As we were all desperately jet-lagged, sitting through a series of briefings did not lend itself to much retention. Yet most of us perked up at the Rules of Engagement brief. The controversy-ridden ROE, as it is called, basically dictates what you can and cannot do in a combat zone—both offensively and defensively. The intent is to protect the soldiers as well as any innocent civilians who may come across them. Contrary to what many may believe, a "shoot first and ask questions later" policy does not exist. The complexities of the ROE gave me that much more respect for the trigger-pullers out there on patrol. I sat there and attempted to imagine being one of those guys at a checkpoint somewhere in the heart of Baghdad, and what it must feel like as a suspicious car rapidly approaches. Within a few seconds, decide that it does not appear the car will stop. Then, the outstretched hand with the shouted Arabic word for halt. And the car continues to barrel toward the checkpoint. The barrel of the M4 is dropped in the direction of the driver...would I pull that trigger or not?

From the briefing area, we humped with our duffle bags to the open bay quarters where we would sleep while at Doha. The thing seemed as big as an airplane hangar—row after row of bunk beds holding hundreds of guys. Some were heading north. Others were on their way home. Many in the lower bunks had attempted to fashion a privacy drape of bath towels and sheets to provide a modicum of solitude in the middle of the former warehouse. I found a bunk and gladly lost consciousness for a few hours.

The next morning we were told that we were soon to be picked up by soldiers from the 256 Brigade, who would drive us out to Camp Buehring where the Brigade was presently staging. We had enough time to obtain our Rapid Fielding Initiative gear before we left. The RFI was an issue of highly desirable equipment such as ballistic sunglasses, an improved combat helmet, even fleece cold weather gear. This was obviously some additional tonnage that no one minded carrying. The last item to procure at Doha was the Interceptor Body Armor (IBA). The IBA is a 16-pound Kevlar vest reinforced in front and behind with Small Arms Protective Insert (SAPI) plates. Despite the heft involved in wearing—and smelling—this thing, it was capable of stopping an AK-47 round, and that was enough for me. It happened to reek as if the previous owner had worn his *at length* [as in the entire year-long deployment] in the desert heat and had never gotten around to cleaning it. I would just have to stink.

I clearly remember how glad I was to see the young enlisted guys from Brigade who had been sent to taxi us out of Camp Doha. It wasn't only because I was so ready to leave Doha's open bays and long lines. I was honestly glad to be around a bunch of Louisianians again—guys with French names and accents more familiar to me than those I had been hearing all week at Fort Bliss. I was sure that in that far away land, it felt like at least a splinter of home.

The Brigade had been heavily involved in preparation for this deployment for months. In May of 2004, it had mobilized to Fort Hood, Texas, home of the Army's 1st Cavalry Division. There, they became skilled in urban operations and close-quarters combat. Cordon and search of a building, security checkpoint operations, convoy support, and even civilian relations—all essential assets in theater—were mastered by the Brigade soldiers. By August, it was time for an encore visit to the National Training Center. Unlike the previous trip in 2001, this trip was a rehearsal exercise to determine readiness for the combat theater. This time, there were no massive movements of tanks against the Kraznovians! By early October, they were on the ground at Camp Buehring in northern Kuwait.

Camp Buehring was a staging base out in the desert, approximately 15 miles from the Iraqi border. Since the beginning of the war, its strategic position had provided an ideal training and preparation point for combat units heading north to Iraq. It was pure desert: wide open, flat, sandy, mightily hot, and draped with endless rows of tents. During their weeks there, the Brigade soldiers had been busy getting ready. Abrams tanks and Bradley fighting vehicles were given final checks. Weapons were sighted-in. Commanders conducted daily meetings to update their subordinates on any changes to the timeline for movement. It was a hopping place by the time we arrived from Doha.

While still trying to adjust to the time and climate changes, we were ushered into a large meeting tent for more—yes—briefings. This time, they were specific to enemy tactics and convoy operations. Specific attention was rightfully given to the infamous improvised explosive device (IED): how it was made, how it was placed, and how it was deployed. The footage that was shown of their detonation and after-effects was incredible—so much destructive power from such a relatively small mechanism. We were then given the obligatory admonition on appropriate water intake, and we were released to our units.

I was picked up by one of First Battalion's sergeants in a humvee and driven out to the complex of tents where they had been billeted. The tents were the elongated crescent type with—I was so glad to see—air conditioners connected to each. I picked a cot inside the one where the Battalion's officers were assigned and cathartically dropped my load of duffel bags. Strangely, despite the fact that the air conditioner was running, it was hardly cooler inside the tent than the balmy 105 degrees outside. Against my better judgment to push through and acclimate to the time change, I elected to flop down on the cot for just a few minutes. I unzipped my CD case, where I had placed one of T.G. McCary's pictures of Melissa and the girls. I could not believe how homesick I had already become—but not too much to keep me from falling asleep immediately.

I awoke nearly two hours later—and still felt drugged. It was time to say hello to all of my guys from the Battalion and to let them know that the doc had arrived. Most of them, I had not seen in months. Between their mobilization training and in-processing at Fort Hood, through a rehearsal exercise at NTC, until now, they had already been gone for nearly six months. Seeing those familiar faces again was an uplifting thing and made me forget about the heat and drowsiness for at least a little while. There was an Internet café nearby, and I was eager to check my email for news from home.

The first email that came up on my inbox was from Melissa, with "granny" as the subject line. My heart sank. Melissa could not have worded her message any better:

"I am sorry to tell you that Granny did die. I am so glad that you were able to talk to her the day before she met Jesus. She died about 8:20 pm Columbus time on Sun. Oct. 17…"

Good for Granny. I fought hard to not really begin feeling sorry for myself, but remembered the lines about strength in the eulogy I had just written— as well as the story of Horatio Spafford. Even still, that was a tough time there in the Camp Buehring Internet Café. I began sending emails to my family, expressing my condolences on our collective loss and to tell them that I had arrived safely in Kuwait. I then made my first call home in the large phone center across the street. Melissa and the girls were fine—

missing me, but otherwise okay. She had informed me in her notification email that she was planning to fly to Ohio to attend the funeral, and I was so grateful that she would be there.

The next day, I got a response from my Uncle David in Ohio, thanking me for the eulogy. His message was as profound and meaningful to me as it was simple. After he had written that Granny was fine now, he ended with, *"Make 'em well over there, doc."* I doubt he realized at the time that this one sentence would become my personal motivating theme for the remainder of my deployment—that in the midst of deep personal loss, the focus was not on self, but on the mission. Regardless of the label: be it "American Spirit," or "Warrior Ethos," it is the mark of selflessness that defines heroes. Reading one email had changed my life.

Things got better over the next few days as I attempted to settle into some type of routine. Fortunately, the regimented pattern of military life is quite conducive to "routine development," and I quickly adjusted. The last remnants of jet lag were gone after about five days, as I forced myself into the new day-night cycle there. I attended daily meetings with Brigade and Battalion staff, where more detailed information about our Area of Responsibility (AOR) was disseminated. Of no less importance were the details about the upcoming movement *to* the AOR. When all the other Brigade docs and I were picked up at Camp Doha, the young enlisted guys who came to get us immediately referred to all of the preparations taking place for this massive road march. One of them then stated, "Y'all probably won't have to go on that. They'll probably chopper the docs into Baghdad." I admit that I had hoped he was right. Riding in a vehicle—armored or not—all the way from Kuwait to Baghdad sounded incredibly perilous—not to mention, long. I preferred to dare the rocket-propelled grenades or shoulder-fired missiles during a short helicopter ride, than to dodge IEDs for three or four days. Alas, I soon learned that there would be no chopper ride. The Brigade commanders had decided that because of the danger involved in this immense movement of vehicles and personnel, having physicians placed strategically throughout the convoy was a needed asset. So be it. I was riding.

That couple of weeks in Kuwait had raced by. In between the ubiquitous nosebleeds that everyone had gotten in the arid heat, vehicles had been up-armored, weapons had been sighted, and convoy operations had been rehearsed. The day prior to our departure, the entire Brigade was called for a formation. Until then, I had never seen a formation any larger than a company-size. This one was immense. A platform had been erected in front, and from it, the Brigade Commander, Brigadier General John Basilica, gave us a final word of encouragement through an electronic megaphone. It was time to go.

By the time every vehicle had been staged in order, they numbered approximately 250, lined up in multiple parallel rows. I would be riding deep somewhere in the middle with a medic from Charlie Company, 199th Forward Support Battalion—otherwise known as "Charlie Med" because of its concentration of medical assets and personnel. 1st Battalion would be escorting all of Charlie Med along the convoy into Iraq.

All of our gear had been cleared from the tent city and loaded onto the vehicles. We would be sleeping on the convoy that night to ensure a precise departure time early the next morning.

That was when I first met the chaplains of the Tiger Brigade. Major Orlando Madrid was a chaplain in the civilian world as well as in the National Guard. He was also from Central Louisiana, where he worked at the federal penitentiary in nearby Pollock. Captain Tyler Wagenmaker was a pastor from Michigan who had been mobilized as the chaplain for 1st Battalion. No dust—or sand—could settle in those guys during that time. I continually observed them darting in and out of the vehicles—praying with some, just talking to others. Some chose to pray in groups with the chaplains. In a time of stress that few there had known previously, they were a stabilizing and encouraging force that only a man of God could provide. And it took the United States Army to display God's love the way He intended it—provision without barrier to race, denomination, or rank. I spoke briefly with Orlando and told him how deeply I appreciated him. I could discern merely by his countenance that he was the real thing, and I was so grateful that he would be there with us. He handed me a paperback soldier's Bible—the sand camo edition—and he went back to work.

Everyone was glad to finally be pulling out of Camp Buehring. We would head from there to the first of three convoy support centers (CSCs) that would serve as rest and refuel points along the way. The first, CSC Navistar, rests just south of the border with Iraq. It was basically a large roadside stop, equipped with a dining facility and an Exchange to allow for a hot meal and any last minute purchases. We would be stopping there for the night and crossing the border in the morning. As we rode forward, the desert north of Camp Buehring, like most of Kuwait, was pure desolation—wide open nothingness. There was nothing but the road, the sand, and the sky. I even saw camel skeletons fossilizing beside the road—if that weren't a statement! Not even a *camel* could make it out there!

Eight

The Cradle Of Civilization

—◦◊◦—

With the relatively slow pace of the convoy, it took a little longer than I had expected to move up to the border. We pulled into Navistar, being careful to maintain the order of sequence, and everyone immediately dashed for the chow hall. Thankfully, the food was provided by the same contractor as we had in Kuwait, so it was all fresh and hot—with very few flies. I made a quick trip afterward to the Exchange and grabbed a mini gooseneck flashlight so I could read a little that night. As the sun set over the desert horizon, I bunked down on one of the litter carriers in the back of the ambulance. I clipped the flashlight to my shirt and turned to the book of Psalms in the little Bible I had gotten earlier from Chaplain Madrid. There was nothing more appropriate that night than the Psalms, with all of David's pleas for protection against approaching enemies. And in each, the mighty protection of God was assured.

The angel of the LORD encamps around those who fear him, and he delivers them.

Psalm 34:7

It was stiflingly hot, but I managed to get a few hours sleep before the early wakeup. Some time before 4:00am, on October 27th, we awoke and the vehicles were started. We had time enough for a quick canteen cup shave and a few bites of an MRE Pop Tart, and the alert call came across the battalion net. Lieutenant Colonel Thomas Plunkett III, 1st Battalion's commander, would lead the convoy, and our convoy would lead the Brigade. 1st Battalion's motto is "First to Fight," and we may have very well been fulfilling it that day. LTC Plunkett issued some final words before the order to move out, and I will never forget them:

"Task Force Geronimo, [a.k.a. 1st Battalion] this is Geronimo Six. Thirteen years ago, I crossed this border to fight these guys. We are about to cross it this morning. Let's go in there and finish the job so that my son doesn't have to come back here again."

He quoted a brief scripture verse and asked for God's blessing and protection upon us all, and the first vehicles began rolling. The lead elements were members of our scout platoon, riding in our most heavily equipped up-armored humvees. I was glad that if I weren't riding in one of those wheeled fortresses, at least the vehicles in front and behind us were well-equipped: the one behind us mounted with an MK-19 automatic grenade launcher, capable of grenade-per-second diplomacy. The one in front of us bore the equally formidable .50 cal. We set out, headed north for the border.

The first major landmark that we would cross would be "The Berm" at the Kuwait-Iraq border. Constructed by the Kuwaitis for obvious historical reasons, the Berm is a 10-foot tall sand barrier complemented by a 15-foot-wide and 15-foot-deep trench that extends from the Persian Gulf to the border with Saudi Arabia. Rows of concertina wire and electrical fencing extend along with it. At least if the Iraqi army ever chose to invade Kuwait again, the border would give them a moment of strategic pause. With the advent of this war, U.S. forces had constructed nine channels through it to allow passage of the invasion force. Soon, the Arabic signs with the familiar red and green horizontal stripes became visible ahead of the concertina wire, and we were crossing over. A Kuwaiti guard opened the gate and observed the passage of yet another fist of American power moving north. At the border, we were ordered to go weapons hot: round in the chamber and safety on. The gunner ahead of us jerked back the bolt on the .50 cal, my driver did the same with his M16, and I followed suit with my pistol.

We would be traveling north on the famed six-lane highway known as Main Supply Route (MSR) Tampa. MSR Tampa is a roughly 600-mile-long artery that extends across Iraq as far as the Syrian border. Historically, it had existed for years, nearly 30 of which, its total paving had remained incomplete. Between multiple wars and shortages in workers and equipment, Saddam had never been able to finish the job. Until its completion in December of 2004 by U.S. and Iraqi cooperation, the MSR was fraught with dust-related accidents. For obvious geographic reasons, it serves as a vital logistical pathway connecting manpower in Iraq to re-supply assets in Kuwait. For obvious *strategic* reasons, it was and is a broad target of insurgent activity. From the placement of IEDs on the roadside or in guardrails, to the bombing of its bridges, the enemy had repeatedly used the MSR to attack its continuous stream of Coalition convoys.

The terrain on both sides of the Berm was nothing short of an historic chronicle of the struggles fought out there since the early nineties. Huge divots dug into the sand had provided concealed fighting positions for Iraqi tanks. Some of the divots still bore the rotting carcass of the Soviet-made T-72s that Iraqi forces used in the invasion of their neighbor to the south. Most remained in the exact dismembered state that the round from the Abrams tanks had left them in years earlier—nothing but a pile of carbonized parts and dust.

A fellow soldier had related a story to me that dates to the Gulf War. With the imminent incursion of American forces from the South, Saddam's Army had dug in to repel their advance. Because of our weapons technology, American tanks were able to detect and fire upon the Iraqi T-72s before they were even aware of their presence. The result was a shockingly lopsided offensive—nearly 4,000 Iraqi tanks destroyed without one American tank lost to enemy fire. Afterward, a surrendering Iraqi tanker reportedly told his captors that his fellow tankers knew the Americans were coming. When queried as to how, his response was, "Because the tanks around us started blowing up!"

We were aware that our journey to Baghdad would increase in potential danger the further north we ventured. Southern Iraq was largely populated by Shiites and Bedouin farmers, neither group ever being fervent Saddam supporters. Subsequently, enemy activity in the south was relatively sparse, and attacks on MSR Tampa there proportionately rare. We still were taking no chances.

The convoy transitioned from the sand to the familiar-looking black pavement of the MSR. Were it not for the stranded, burned-out vehicles and nearby flocks of camels, it could have easily been mistaken for I-15 through Nevada. As we eased north, the void of the Kuwaiti desert gradually gave way to palm trees and grass; I had forgotten what dirt looked like over the past several days. And it was the same dirt that actually formed the homes of the Bedouin farmers we began to encounter—ancient peoples scratching a subsistence out of goat herding. They lived in mud shacks, wore flowing robes, and drew their water from canals. I absolutely felt as if I were taking a drive through some Old Testament tour at a theme park somewhere in Florida; it was a place that had hardly moved out of "B.C." in 2000 years. Their children would occasionally stand at the roadside, waving their hands or lifting a thumbs up: all in an effort to snag a thrown gift from a soldier. By the time of our convoy, Iraqi children had grown accustomed to a Mardi Gras experience each time a humvee passed: soccer balls, MREs, even ink pens were rare commodities, and the kids went plain berserk over them.

In addition to being stressful, the convoy was physically grueling. First—of course—it was as predictably hot as always, and there was no A/C in the crackerbox ambulance—only the kind that blew in the armored windows as we cruised along. The passenger's seat was set an exact 90-degree angle with the backrest, and the seat cushion was about an inch worth of foam rubber that warmed from the engine. I had over-adjusted my Kevlar helmet so that the band was too tight on my scalp. So after an hour, I was sweltering under my uniform and had a contiguous head, rear-end, and backache for which there was no end in sight. Looking back, I think the only thing that kept me from losing it was the intense distraction that IED avoidance provided. My eyes were stuck on the roadside, and I made sure my head stayed behind the cut piece of steel over my door. I remembered the words of the Psalms and prayed. Again and again.

Our mid-way stop would be at another CSC. This time: CSC Cedar II. By late afternoon, we had arrived there without incident. Port-a-potties, food, rest: in *that* particular order.

Interestingly, the food that night was even a little better than the meal we had eaten the night before at Navistar. We had been told to expect that: the further north, seemingly the better the eats. There was a huge hot food line, a monster salad bar, soft drinks, desserts (even hand-dipped milkshakes). I was trying to imagine what we would have in Baghdad—steak and lobster? It was interesting to meet fellow soldiers from participating Coalition countries while we were there. Most of them were British, a few were Estonian, and some were Korean.

The Brits were easy enough to spot even *out* of their unique uniforms with their tasseled berets and distinct camouflage pattern. They quite evidently were not forced to abide by the same appearance guidelines that American service members are expected to maintain; shaggy hair and mismatched T-shirts and shorts were common. I even saw a few Brits walking from a shower facility back to their tent in nothing but a wrapped-around towel and flip-flops! Should an American soldier attempt something convenient like that in a tactical environment, he would soon find himself nose-to-nose with a highly displeased command sergeant major. Uniform discipline is a must. But irrespective of their sartorial shortcomings, everybody liked the Brits. Sharing a meal with them and swapping unit patches made everyone forget about the growing threat of our journey, if at least for a little while.

The next morning was the same routine as before: rise with the sun, and prepare to ride. Thankfully, the next stop would be the last CSC before Baghdad. I had left home for Fort Bliss, Fort Bliss for Camp Doha, Camp Doha for Camp Buehring, Camp Buehring for Navistar, Navistar for Cedar II, and now would be headed from Cedar II to CSC Scania. As one who finds comfort in the stability of routine, I had become bone-weary of transience.

The transformation of the land continued even more as we approached Scania. The last vestiges of frank desert had given way to the alluvial plain of the Fertile Crescent. The soil became darker, the palms became more numerous, dense reeds and cattails lined canals feeding water from the Euphrates to the ubiquitous agricultural demand of the surrounding area. I hearkened back to my Western Civilization class at Louisiana College 13 years earlier and the details of this key region of the world: the land of Mesopotamia, Abraham, and Babylon—the Cradle of Civilization indeed. Could I have ever imagined that a day would come when I would be zooming through it on a paved road at 60mph, just trying not to get blown up? Hardly.

CSC Scania. When we arrived there, we were a mere 60 miles south of Baghdad. Everyone was keenly aware that the next and final leg of our journey would be the most perilous. The incidence of IED attacks there had been detailed even before leaving Camp Buehring, and the vigilance level would be intense. Everyone tried to decompress a bit by exploring Scania—hitting the Exchange or dining facility (yes, it was even better than Cedar II). We were not the only convoy passing through Scania that day, and we were staged close to all of the others.

The nearest was comprised of heavy trucks taking all kinds of vehicles and equipment to Kuwait. I saw a crowd of my guys congregating around one of the trucks on whose bed rested the remains of an up-armored humvee. It had very obviously been struck by an IED and was sheared into a gnarled fist of steel and glass. We all knew how formidable the armoring was on those things, and that one looked as if it could have just as well been a Ford Pinto™. The interior was even more disturbing. Blood and tissue had been sprayed all over the dash and windshield, and a large pool had dried on the driver's seat. It was our first actual—albeit indirect—contact with the brutal reality that we faced there. Everyone was silent. Some snapped pictures. I did not. It was a good time to call home.

It had to have been in the middle of the night when I called, but Melissa had told me to call when I could, regardless of the time. Operations Security, or OPSEC as it is called, is a term given to the protection of tactical information that could potentially be intercepted and used by the enemy. It was closely monitored on phone calls home, and we were prohibited from discussing exact locations, departure times, etc. I simply told Melissa that I was fine, that I loved her, and to remind everyone to pray. They knew we were on our way, and that was enough. God would handle the details.

Sleep was an intermittent and superficial thing that night for us all. I think when the wakeup call finally came, we were all relieved to be confronting this challenge. The chaplains were back at it—making their rounds up and down the convoy, offering quick words of encouragement and prayer. Several groups, even without the chaplain, were huddling up for prayer. One of my favorite pictures from that morning was a shot taken by one of my medics as he stood on the hood of a humvee, looking down on a group of guys praying. And it was not just any group of guys. It was the scout platoon: the head of the convoy, the tip of the spear. These were not a bunch of manicurists and interior decorators. These were the some of the craziest, hard-chargers in the Brigade, and in this critical hour, they were making the Call. *That* is the spirit of the American soldier. With the escorts from the 1st Cavalry Division in place to guide us in to Camp Victory, it was time to roll out one final time. With the rumble of diesel engines starting, I read what I felt was the most appropriate Psalm. I had known it since I was a child in Sunday School, but that morning in Central Iraq, I understood David's words all the more.

The LORD [is] my shepherd; I shall not want.
He maketh me to lie down in green pastures:
he leadeth me beside the still waters.
He restoreth my soul:
he leadeth me in the paths of righteousness
for his name's sake.
Yea, though I walk through the valley of
the shadow of death,
I will fear no evil: for thou [art] with me; thy rod
and thy staff they comfort me.
Thou preparest a table before me in
the presence of mine enemies:

thou anointest my head with oil;
my cup runneth over.
Surely goodness and mercy shall follow me
all the days of my life:
and I will dwell in the house
of the LORD for ever.

—Psalm 23 KJV

We locked and loaded. The convoy began uneventfully as before, and we all quickly accelerated to cruising speed on the MSR. As we inched closer to Baghdad, overpasses and checkpoints became more prevalent. I watched closely as our gunners ducked on approaching an overpass, and then spun around backwards to monitor the backside. In doing so, they avoided the decapitating wires that insurgents were known to hang and prevented any attempt to drop grenades off the bridge for the next vehicle.

There were no headaches, backaches, or any other aches for that matter on this trip. It was all focus. Every foot—every second—brought us that little bit closer to "safety." I continued to pray—one, two sentences at a time. Every few miles, we would ride over a splatter of soot shooting out across the road. Many were centered by a marked absence of a huge chunk of pavement. And of course, we all knew what had happened *right there* at some point. After seeing more and more of those IED scars paraded past us, I found myself gradually growing more uneasy and anxious for the trip to be over. I know I wasn't the only one. I found myself praying in more than one or two sentences, and more often than earlier. It was then that I got an answer.

The diesel engine of the ambulance was quite loud at that speed, and the hum of the big tires chimed right in. Moreover, my ears were jammed with a pair of fat ballistic earplugs. As a result, I couldn't clearly make out the odd sound that I could perceive coming behind us. It was a deep, clipped rumble, but was too high to be on the ground and was not coming in fast enough to be a jet. The wind had picked up and had stirred a cloud of the famously dense dirt and sand into the air so the visibility was almost as poor. Yet, it became louder, and I strained to look out of the side mirrors.

In an instant, the dust was blasted outward, and through it leaped a pair of AH-64 Apache attack helicopters, flying parallel on each side of the MSR. Both were rocketing to the front of the convoy, tilted forward at 45 degrees, barely 100 feet from the ground. I had seen Apaches before—plastic models, photographs; I had even seen actual choppers parked on a tarmac. What I had never seen was a head-on view of one in flight, with the Hellfire missiles, Hydra rockets, and 30mm cannon pointing *at* me in the mirror. They are a steel embodiment of pure, unadulterated destruction, and they were there to obliterate anyone brave enough to take their chances against us. They reached the front of the convoy and turned back around to fly to the rear. I recalled a story my grandmother had related to me as a child—about the "goodness and mercy" of the 23rd Psalm actually representing angels whom God sends to protect us from the enemy. Before that day on the convoy, I had imagined a pair of 10-foot-tall brilliant angels, swords raised, flying on each side of our ambulance up the MSR. As we approached Baghdad, I guess God wanted to confirm that for us: Goodness on one side, Mercy on the other.

A sign soon became visible about a fourth of a mile ahead: a large blue and green metal one hanging from a steel frame as if it were a highway in the States. Pointing right to the approaching exit, it read "Baghdad Airport."

Nine

Stand Up

—◦◦◦—

October 29, 2004. We jubilantly veered off of MSR Tampa and onto the reed-lined road to Camp Victory. Victory was a sprawling installation southwest of Baghdad, adjacent to the former Saddam International Airport—now Baghdad International Airport (BIAP). After the fall of Baghdad, the area was converted to the vast main center of operations for the war, with a capacity of roughly 14,000 troops. Its focal point was the awe-inspiring Al Faw Palace, built by Saddam to commemorate some ostensibly significant victory over Iran during the Iran-Iraq War. Scattered throughout the rest of Victory were man-made lakes, around which a myriad of "subordinate" palaces had also been built.

The Brigade would be taking over a subdivision of Victory that had formerly housed the 1st Cavalry Division's 2nd Brigade Combat Team, a.k.a. "Blackjack." As was typically the custom, the area had been named "Camp Blackjack" after its occupying unit. With a few more months remaining in Blackjack's year-long rotation, they unfortunately were relocated to a tent city across Victory prior to our arrival. I am quite sure that they were not passionate fans of the 256 Brigade as they settled into those tents, and the Camp Blackjack sign was replaced with one declaring it "Camp Tiger."

Camp Tiger was, for all intents and purposes, a self-sufficient community. Multiple clusters of residential trailers were supported by a large pay phone facility, a barber shop, a laundry drop-off [yes, laundry was a contract service], exercise facility, and even a small "hajji mart." Hajji marts are the bazaar-type markets run by local Iraqis. They sell everything from cellular phones to hookahs and are amazingly popular among soldiers. Just down the road from all of these amenities was the expansive dining facility—also run by contract services. The food there was resoundingly good. This was not the "mess tent" of the old war movies: no fat guy in a stained, hole-ridden tank top slinging goopy gravy onto an amorphous hash cake. There were eggs-to-order every morning, fresh fruit and salads, and hand-dipped milkshakes. Unless guys were patrolling in the field, and thus relegated to the packaged surprises of the MRE, food would not be a source of discomfort at Camp Tiger. And on the road from the DFAC back to the residential area, a sign was posted amid the rolls of concertina wire, reading: "Be polite, be professional, be prepared to kill."

1st Battalion's Aid Station would be set up in one side of a residential trailer, and we stood up ready to operate almost immediately. Two patient litters were set up against two of the walls, propped horizontally to serve as "beds." Medicines ranging from ibuprofen all the way up to ICU-grade intravenous antibiotics were stored in a cabinet on the other side of the room. We were equipped for anything from the dime-a-dozen sprain to a respiratory arrest requiring intubation. I certainly hoped that much dust would collect on the equipment for the latter.

The physician's assistant (PA) was First Lieutenant Jeff McCorcle, who had arrived at the Battalion not too long after I had joined the Guard. Jeff was a real gem of a military PA. Prior to joining the National Guard, he had been an active duty senior noncommissioned officer in the Army. After completing PA school, Jeff took a position in the Burn Unit at Brook Army Medical Center at Fort Sam Houston. There he had become skilled in the complexities of critical care as it pertained to trauma and major burn recovery — so much that he was actually a foremost trainer of medical students and surgical residents who rotated through his unit. Jeff's set of skills in Iraq was just perfect; he knew the workings of the Army and how to handle battle injuries. What's more, I really liked the guy. For this, I was indeed thankful. As we would be working together day in and out for the next few months, any contentiousness could have made for one miserable experience.

With our medic platoon leader, First Lieutenant Jason Warren, tasked out for various needs throughout the Battalion, Jeff assumed a lot of the coordination duties. Allotments of medics to the line companies, as well as round-the-clock staffing of the aid station, had to be immediately established, and Jeff was key in ordering all of the moving parts. The medics were immediately positioned in each spot where they were needed, bringing the Battalion that much closer to readiness for combat operations. Heaven knows that if it had been up to me, our medics would have been lucky to be Band-Aid-capable.

The military's official reporting time to receive routine medical attention is referred to as sick call, and ours would take place seven days per week at 7:00am and again at 4:00pm. Soldiers would report to sick call for routine medical issues while we remained constantly on call for emergencies. Should anything come through the door that exceeded our capabilities, the Brigade Aid Station was practically within sight, along with its evacuation assets. The Brigade-level clinic was staffed by the other doctors with whom I had mobilized. It was a large fixed facility with multiple treatment beds and a medical hold area where soldiers could be treated for days, if needed. From there, choppers could be called in to rapidly transport soldiers to the Combat Support Hospital in Baghdad's famed Green Zone. The "CASH," as it was known, was the medical grand central station for all of the military's serious medical needs in the vicinity of Baghdad, and that's saying a lot. Any gunshot wound, IED blast, or illness that exceeded the capabilities of the combat unit level was headed there in a Blackhawk. Stabilizing treatment was provided, and if needed, air transport to Germany or the States. I would later hear from guys who had spent a few days in medical hold at the CASH that the chopper noise was virtually incessant, with incoming and outgoing traffic around the clock—a sobering barometer of the reality of this war.

My first night in the trailer at Camp Tiger was a memorable one. With a temporary shortage of furniture, the earliest arrivals had cannibalized from other trailers to address the deficiencies of their own. In other words, in a trailer that should have held a bed and a footlocker, I opened a door to four walls and a dirty floor. Yet, after weeks of open bay accommodations and sultry tents, I was *delighted* with a private room and window unit. I was able to procure a cot, upon which my newly issued sleeping beg was spread, and I was, as they say in the Army, "good to go." Obviously paranoid, I oriented the cot with my feet in front of the trailer's door so that I had instant visibility of anyone trying to become an uninvited guest. Despite the reality that I was in an incredibly fortified installation with multiple tiers of security, I was overly mindful of the abduction stories I had heard on the news. I was taking no chances. Just before clicking out my overhead fluorescent light, I performed one last task: ramming a loaded magazine into my M9 pistol and cocking a round into the chamber. It would be my cot partner for the first several days in Iraq.

It didn't take long to run into Stuart West. The second day at the camp, as I was dropping off several days' worth of dirty clothes at the laundry depot, I found him leaving the nearby hajji mart with one of his soldiers. It was a warm reunion. There we were, in the heart of the Middle East, covered in camouflage and Kevlar, with weapons at our sides. How could he have ever known that one simple phone call could have led to that moment? I hoped that he was not regretful, and I assured him accordingly. We took a picture to commemorate the moment and went our separate ways.

I would later hear an apt characterization of a soldier's life in Iraq as *Groundhog Day,* referencing the popular comedy movie in which Bill Murray lives the same day over and over. The routine is in fact largely that: performing the same inventories of tasks and responsibilities without respect to the day of the week or the particular holiday of the year. I have always found that routine expedited the passage of time, and I surely welcomed it in this case. In the previous few weeks, marked by a continuous stream of upheavals and relocations, putting on a stethoscope and writing prescriptions grounded me in something deeply familiar. I was living my dream, carrying out God's mission—only now that mission had taken me to the epicenter of all things bad in the world.

Our first few weeks in-country were relatively uneventful from a combat perspective. Oddly, the predominant presenting complaint to our aid station was...diarrhea. Certainly, there were adequate numbers of orthopedic and dermatologic issues, just as at the NTC, but *diarrhea*? And this stretched across the Brigade, seemingly without explanation. The drinking water was bottled. All of the food was meticulously prepared and served by the contract service. Hand washing was strictly enforced anyway. It almost became amusing as our soldiers would sheepishly enter the aid station with a sick call slip. When the medic asked them what they were there for, the answer would typically be the outstretched slip with the complaint written on it. Most of these tough guys were not overly proud to have to go to sick call in the first place. To be going for a bad case of diarrhea was major ego deflator.

From a medical standpoint, this was my first experience with the often divergent clinical guidelines between Army and civilian medicine. I had been taught—as most infectious disease references advise—that with most cases of diarrhea, when there is neither fever nor blood present in the stool, that a virus is the cause. Accordingly, the course is usually self-limited and will resolve on its own in two to three days. In Iraq however, official treatment recommendations formulated at high echelons of medical command advised something much more aggressive. Essentially assuming these cases were due to food-borne illness, broad-spectrum antibiotics were advised in the first three days. By the time the diarrhea surge was over a few weeks later, we had resorted to assembling "diarrhea packs": one medicine bag with the ciprofloxacin antibiotic pills and the second bag with the antidiarrheal du jour.

By the second month, diarrhea gave way to an infirmity that came to be known by many names, some of which are unsuitable for print. The most memorable to me was the "Kuwaiti Crud," so-named because of its predominance among soldiers arriving there. The Kuwaiti Crud—or more aptly, acute bronchitis—was a respiratory condition marked by severe cough and mild bronchiole spasm: components of a typical asthma attack. Unlike the first month's illness of choice, the source of the bronchitis was no mystery. To put it mildly, the EPA had not yet become involved in the air pollution guidelines for countries in Southwest Asia. Between the sand and dirt kicked into the air by the high heat and winds, and the ubiquitous burning of all sorts of industrial and domestic waste, the sky seemed to stay a murky brown. At night, a laser pointer could be directed upward, and the thin red beam that would normally be invisible in clean air, could be visualized as a ruby ice pick hundreds of feet into the particulate-filled sky. And again in this case, antibiotics were advised early in the treatment course. The aim was clear in both: providing soldiers the most expedient means of disease resolution so that they could return to health, and the mission would continue. The sooner the mission was complete, the sooner we would all be home.

Ten

Three Months In Iraq

＝◡◡◡＝

After negotiating the perils of diarrhea and bronchitis, we had attempted to find some relative degree of normalcy. The pace of operations remained high for our guys, and with it, the increased risk of casualties. The patrols and checkpoints were manned around the clock, every day, without respect to the weather or day of the week. Dating as far back as the Civil War, conditions were largely characterized as boredom interrupted by sheer terror. I found that axiom to hold true—for myself and the guys I took care of.

Minor injuries from the infamous IED began to trickle in. Guys would recall stories of driving along a patrol zone that they had traversed scores of times earlier when—boom! Their hulking humvees would be launched into the air. Smoke would blind them, and the concussion would render everything silent. Thankfully, most of the injuries were minor: bruises, sprains, and perforated eardrums. Some were more involved when the shrapnel from the blast found an opening in the vehicle or if the soldier—usually a gunner—was exposed. Often if the shrapnel was small and in a non-critical area, it would be left alone rather than risk a surgical complication. Regardless, I seemed to find that nearly all of the guys were eager to get back on patrol. Since they were always confined to quarters in the first few days after the injury, they were required to be seen in the aid station for reassessment each day. By three days of nothing but a bunk and four walls, most of them were anxious to the point of misery. Every encounter with them ended with the rather predictable question to me: "Sir, when can I get back with my guys?" I learned a lesson on healing from those soldiers that rivaled those I had picked up in the halls of Charity Hospital.

Shortly after our arrival, night operations began in our sector. I would soon learn that with it came the occasional need for tactical illumination of a particular area. I was in the habit of going to bed around 10:00, and by 11:30 on that particular night, I was in a veritable coma. I struggle to describe the power of the explosion that awoke me. We have all been startled awake by a noise in the house—usually something falling off a counter or a telephone ringing in the wee hours. Despite the often trivial source, the result can be profound, with the racing heart, the cold sweat, and the sense of utter terror.

What I had not known as I fell asleep earlier was that there was a planned firing of illumination rounds from the 155mm howitzers emplaced down the road from us. These howitzers are capable of easily sending rounds over ten miles away, so the amount of power necessary to do so is considerable. BOOM! The report from the first round rattled the entire camp. The thin walls of the trailer quaked. The bed moved. I was certain that we had just been mortared. As I frantically prepared to throw on my uniform and head to the aid station to receive casualties, another one went off. BOOM! I cracked the door of my trailer to see everyone around me doing the same. The message gradually drifted back to us from those in the know that these were in fact "outgoing illum' rounds." I felt like an idiot. It took me three hours for the adrenaline to wear off so I could get back to sleep.

The next morning, as I was examining one of out soldiers who had recently been in an IED blast, I sheepishly related my reaction to the previous night's fireworks.

He laughed. "Don't feel bad, sir! I was on the floor low crawling to get under the bed!"

The excitement continued a few days later when our 1LT Warren returned to the aid station from a battalion staff meeting. I could read from the half-committed smile in my direction that I might not be happy about what he would soon tell me. Apparently one of the battalion's companies had encountered an Iraqi family in their sector that had a chronically ill baby. In the ongoing battle for the hearts and minds of the Iraqi people, the company commander had offered to bring an American doctor to evaluate the child. LTC Plunkett had agreed that it was a good idea and ordered the mission for the next day. This was not done flippantly. Sending a physician outside the wire was a risky exposure of a scarce combat asset, and it would be my first since coming in the gate weeks earlier. I elected to not say anything about this to Melissa that night—better that she know after the fact, than be worried until my next call.

I would link up with CPT Jody Guidry and his soldiers the next morning at 8:00am. After sick call, I loaded my magazine, grabbed my Kevlar, strapped on my IBA and headed down to meet them. They were already waiting. Guidry greeted me warmly and directed me to the rear seat in his up-armored humvee. The doors slammed shut with a thud. Everything about those things just absolutely glared of indestructibility, and I could not imagine the lethality of a force that could destroy them. We were the lead vehicle in a patrol convoy that included two other humvees and an M113. As we made our way through the gate, all magazines were clicked in place and rounds chambered. The .50 cal gunner standing in the hatch scanned the horizon for any threats lurking in the reeds. But it wasn't the threat on two legs that I feared; it was the buried one with the little wires leading away from it that I was more concerned with.

We were quickly out in the countryside surrounding Victory—all farmland carved up by canals running in all directions. As we barreled down the dirt road, CPT Guidry would bark an order to the driver about every 30 seconds relative to his speed and the distance from the vehicle behind him. When he wasn't doing that, he was on the radio, directing the guys in the rear vehicles. After 15 minutes of that stressful exchange, we pulled down a dirt alley that led to a residence. It was typical of the Iraqi homes in that area: boxy, made of mud brick, with bars on the windows. As is custom, the men and boys came out to greet us; the women remained out of sight. CPT Guidry jumped out and began directing traffic, ordering a cordon and search of the home. One of the humvees remained with us. The other one accompanied the 113 around the side of the house as its occupants dismounted. Within seconds, there was a perimeter of M16s and .50cals pointing outward. The soldiers in the humvee behind us had already greeted the Iraqis and had entered the home with CPT Guidry to ensure its safety. Two minutes later, the call came to my driver, "Okay, we're clear. We're coming for the doc."

In 1996, President Clinton had flown to Alexandria to ceremonially hand over control of the former England Air Force Base to the city. Melissa and I had been selected with several other students from Louisiana College to drive cars in his motor-cade—cars filled with Secret Service and press agents. At the conclusion of the day, the reward was a handshake with the President. Some images in life are indelible, and that was one. The door opened at the back of the Pentecostals of Alexandria church where he had been, and out jumped two suited Secret Service agents. Behind them came the man himself, and one memorable handshake.

Another seemingly more indelible image mate-rialized now as those two soldiers came out of the front door of that Iraqi house—to escort me in. There I was, flanked by two infantry soldiers with M16s and surrounded by even more. I had no idea I was that important, but was grateful for the gesture. I was also sure that Melissa would appreciate knowing that if I were outside the wire, at least I was afforded aggressive security.

The Iraqi home was sparsely furnished, with one sofa in the living area. A straw rug covered what may very well have been a dirt floor. The men rose to shake my hand and proclaimed the standard "As-salaam alaykum"—"Peace be with you" in Arabic. The man in the center of the room held a toddler, and all attention quickly gravitated toward him. CPT Guidry handed me a stack of papers that were obviously the child's medical records, with a mixture of Arabic and English on the mostly typed pages. Fortunately, the most crucial pages were the English ones, and they indicated that the child was suffering from a rare inborn metabolic dysfunction known as a glycogen storage disease. In this case, an enzymatic deficiency was leading to the gradual failure of his liver. And there was probably nothing that could be done to reverse it. Despite his young age, the records reflected marked cellular destruction of the liver, as confirmed by a biopsy that he had undergone months earlier. Indeed, this was no Third World evaluation.

As I examined the baby, the room fell silent, and I could sense 20 pairs of eyes fixed upon this child and me. His father held him in his lap as I listened to his heart and lungs and felt the lower edge of his markedly distended liver. I could only imagine what these people were hoping I would say through our interpreter. They had to be hoping that the omnipotent American doctor would recognize a gap in the diagnostic workup and prescribe just the right medicine that would make their baby well again—or at least delay the grim inevitability of the disease process. There just wasn't that medicine, even at the greatest academic medical centers in the States. The first thing I did was assure the family that the evaluation had been excellent, but that there was typically no cure for this type of disease. At the time, one of the other doctors across Victory was a pediatric gastro-enterologist, and I advised the family that I would discuss the case with him on my return.

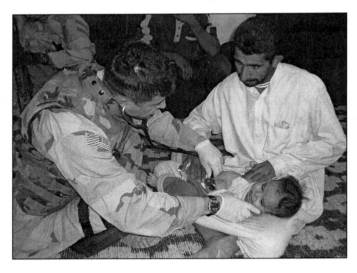

The tears and disappointment I expected did not come. Instead, there were only handshakes, right hands placed on the heart, and "shukran"—"Thank you" in Arabic. Just as if we were leaving our own family, they all piled out in their driveway to wave and see us off. Despite the enormity of our differences: geographical, cultural, religious, economic, some things are always common. One such thing will always be the love of children and the willingness to traverse any difficulty for their well-being. That day I had encountered a family of Iraqis who were willing to have Coalition vehicles parked in their driveway, knowing they could subsequently be targeted by insurgents, in the hope that healing might come for their baby. As we drove away, I hoped that somehow, someday, it would.

By Thanksgiving, I was as well-adapted to life in Iraq as I guessed I could be. The stream of mail from home was wonderfully steady, as were the care packages that came from so many friends and family members. I had accumulated a convenience store's inventory of snacks and baby wipes, had a personal coffee maker, and had wallpapered my room with pictures from home. And on one wall was an American flag that I had bought at the PX. In addition to the pictorial reminders of those for whom I was fighting, I also felt it important to have a reminder of *what* I was fighting for—nothing like a little star spangled encouragement. That flag will always be special to me.

Thanksgiving Day, like any other day there, started with the same routine. The food service contractors had constructed a huge wooden Mayflower replica in front of the dining hall, and the inside was fully decorated. Beyond pilgrim and Indian cutouts hanging from the ceiling tiles, they had cloth-covered the tables and chairs. Reception-style fountains were filled with a sparkling punch, and the menu was all-out Thanksgiving. They had even gotten some of our guys to supervise the making of a Louisiana jambalaya! I guess word had spread around Victory; when the doors opened for lunch, the line stretched for over a quarter mile. As I exited afterward, an ABC camera crew was filming Thanksgiving messages for their morning show, and I shot one to give Melissa and the girls the obligatory "I love you, and I'll be home soon" message. (I had always wanted to do that!)

I agree with the axiom that the positive is under-reported in Iraq, and I understand why. Explosions and casualties are the stuff of headlines. Lives saved every day from just getting the job done hardly sell papers or spark discussion on the Sunday talk shows. Such a story occurred in mid-December while I was there—a story that I am quite sure never made it back to the States.

On the 13th, one of 1st Battalion's patrols was underway in a nearby farming area that interestingly had been owned by Saddam's son, Udai. At one point, one of our guys identified an incongruous black Suburban parked by a lone farmhouse. As they headed for the house, a group of men bolted out from inside, abandoning the Suburban. The SUV was of the type typically used by security forces to escort political officials, and it was oddly out of place that far from the city. But peering in the back revealed the big surprise. A large metallic orb was hunkered in the rear compartment with wires leading away from it: the Suburban was clearly intended to be a vehicle-born IED, and one that would be aimed at a very high-profile target. We soon learned that the orb was in fact an anti-ship bomb, the explosive power of which could have killed scores of people.

I later attended the pinning ceremony where the members of that unit received commendations. Lieutenant General Pete Chiarelli, the Commanding General of the 1st Cavalry Division, came to personally pin those guys and offer his words of congratulations. His message was clear: without the diligence and awareness of this group of soldiers, the likely result would have indeed been catastrophic. And *that* would have made headlines.

LTG Chiarelli wasn't the only high profile face to pass through during my stay there. With the generous attention directed at the war and our central geographic location on a large installation, a veritable list of generals, pro athletes, actors, and politicians made the trip there, just during my short stay. One night, I entered the dining facility to find a flurry of activity around a reconfigured group of tables at the front of the dining room. Digital cameras were snapping, and people I had never seen dressed in civilian clothes frenzied about, trying to look dreadfully busy. I did recognize the people in the center of the crowd, shaking hands and posing for pictures. The first face was Senator Mitch McConnell of Kentucky. The next was our own Senator Mary Landrieu. Following, were Senators Norm Coleman and then Senate Majority Leader and fellow physician Bill Frist. In addition to doling out some backslaps and attaboys to the soldiers, the senators were there to meet with LTG Chiarelli and assess the current status of the war from a ground commander. I admit that it was a bit surreal to be scooping croutons and thousand island dressing at a salad bar next to a United States Senator, as I did with Senator McConnell, but after all, we were both Americans in this foreign land, serving a common purpose.

I ate with some of my medics at a table nearby so we could observe the exciting twist to our normal dinner routine. For much of their meal, they sat huddled toward the table with the General at the center, seeming to hang intently on everything he was telling them. At the conclusion of their dinner meeting, the lawmakers rose and shuffled through the dining room, shaking hands and taking pictures. I even snatched a couple with Senators Landrieu and Frist—special mementos to my tour in Iraq. Weeks after the senators came Robin Williams, John Elway, and even then-Chairman of the Joint Chiefs of Staff General Richard Myers. The celebrity visits were always announced in advance, but the political and military VIPs, for obvious reasons, were surprise affairs. I soon began carrying my digital camera just like I did my wallet and my weapon!

As the weeks ticked toward Christmas, I grew ever anxious to be at home. The weather in Iraq became even more inhospitable, with frequent rains and temperatures dipping into the 40s—hardly the constant heat and sand that I had expected. All the Bing Crosby and Nat King Cole songs in the world made little difference. It was still not home. Melissa had sent me a miniature pre-lit Christmas tree that took residence on top of my footlocker, and I wall-papered my wood paneling with cards and pictures from home. In the pay phone room, I could hear the same yearning in the guys all around me.

As the holidays approached, and the desire to be with family deepened, the conversations became less animated—quieter, deeper, more profound. There was the occasional restrained sniffle, which became less occasional as the days passed. They were tough times. Two days before Christmas, I had just left sick call to check email at the Internet café, only to find it oddly closed at that time of the day. That was likely a bad sign, as phone and computer access would cease only in the event of a casualty—allowing the Army to contact family members before calls or emails began flying homeward. As I approached the battalion TOC, it was obvious that my suspicions were true. Faces were grim, and the normal bustle inside was decidedly muted. Command Sergeant Major Steve Stuckey greeted me with the news that the battalion had indeed suffered its first casualty. A devastatingly powerful IED had been detonated near one of our patrolling humvees—punching a molten wad of metal straight through its armor and into the rear passenger compartment. Three of the four guys inside escaped relatively unharmed, but the young lieutenant in the back was killed instantly. The lethal inevitability of this war had finally met the 256 Brigade, as we all knew that it would. I was in the aid station when the lieutenant's Kevlar helmet and uniform were brought in. The seemingly indestructible helmet was splintered and deformed from the impact. Dark bits of tissue were still inside it. The uniform itself was splattered with blood, as were the boots. Images from the Accident Room at Charity Hospital flashed back to me at that moment. None compared to what was before me now. It was all reverently placed on one of the exam tables, and the medics and I just stood in silence. There was nothing to say.

People at home thought I was joking when I told them that we ate steak and lobster on Christmas Day in Iraq. We really did. I guess they were expecting something like turkey loaf and green beans drowning in cream of mushroom soup, but the meal was a great consolation prize. It was a steel-gray, rainy day—quite fitting to the general sentiment. And apart from the meal and the green/red décor in the dining hall, Christmas was business as usual in the Global War on Terror. Patrols ran. Bad guys were chased. Weapons were fired. Because of the elevated threat of a mortar attack on a Christian holiday, we were ordered to wear Kevlar and IBA even while on Victory — just in case of one lucky shot over the wall. For those of us who were fortunate enough to be able to call home, it was cheering to hear of what Santa had dropped down the chimney and how everyone at home wished for our presence. I took comfort in the fact that I would be with them all soon.

The weeks closing my deployment were hardly uneventful as the anticipation to leave grew. In yet another attempt to reach out to the population in our sector, I was ordered out to examine an injured Iraqi lady. Because of her family's cooperation with our patrolling forces, insurgents had seen fit to mortar their home. None of the family had been seriously injured, but the matriarch had been struck in the hand by a piece of shrapnel. They had initially sought medical attention at a Baghdad hospital where the metal fragment had been removed, but her pain had persisted — so much so, that the family had reported it to our patrol.

As soon as I laid eyes on the poor lady, it was glaringly obvious that she was miserable. The thumb was crudely wrapped in a filthy dressing that I carefully removed to reveal a puffy sausage of a thumb that she was unable to move at all. The shrapnel wound had actually healed nicely, but something was clearly still wrong. As I kept shooting questions back and forth through our interpreter, one of the lady's sons walked up behind me with an X-ray film in his hand—the actual pre-removal film that had been shot at the Iraqi hospital. I lifted the film to the only view box available: a west-facing window. Through the waning sunlight, I could easily see the chunk of shrapnel butting against the first metatarsal of her right hand, but as I scrutinized it more closely, a hairline fracture of the bone was visible underneath. It had apparently been missed at the hospital, and the lady had been sent home with nothing to stabilize the healing bone. One of my medics whipped out his trauma case, and a splint was placed on the thumb two minutes later. We all achieved instant hero status in the eyes of that brave family. I only hoped that they were heartened in their support of our efforts in their country—that freedom was a worthy risk.

That night, I sat outside of my trailer in a folding chair with a cup of Christmas present coffee and stared up at the clear winter sky. I was listening to a Steven Curtis Chapman song from a CD that I had picked up while I was still at Camp Buehring. The song, titled "Believe Me Now," is God reminding his children of his faithfulness during dangerous times vis-à-vis an allusion to Moses at the Red Sea. While I was certainly not standing before an ocean with the rumble of an angry Egyptian army at my back, I had no doubt felt the enemy on all sides of me on more than one occasion. But the song triumphantly climaxes with the following lyric:

I never have, I never will abandon you. And the God that I have always been, I will forever be, so believe me now.

Through welling tears, I gazed at stars that were twinkling down on my family halfway across the world, and I thanked God for His provision. Even now, that song moves me in deep places, and it will always be a reminder to me of God's presence in the darkest times. Whatever the circumstance, nothing can defy His rescue ability.

Nearly four months had passed. I was ready to be a civilian again. And a regular doctor. And a husband. And a daddy. With but a few days remaining in my rotation, I was called to a battalion staff meeting—something that had also become part of my weekly routine. There, LTC Plunkett, flanked by his staff and company commanders, was briefed on the current operational status. Either Jeff McCorcle or I would give a quick detail on the numbers reporting to sick call, their dispositions, and any trends of which the Command should be alerted. On this final meeting for me, the S1, CPT Lance Magee, concluded the meeting with "Doc, front and center." (Not the usual jump to attention and "First to Fight" salute that was normally observed.) I stood at attention in front of the Commander as the orders for my first medal were read. Even though the Army Commendation Medal was one of the Army's more common awards, it was still my first, and I was honored to have been thought of that way by so many whom I regarded as true American heroes. After he had pinned the green ribbon on my breast pocket, the call was issued around the room for "speech." I thanked them all for their support over the previous months and commended them on their unyielding patriotism. Quite simply, the honor had been mine to have even been among them.

The Day arrived. All of the physician replacements had, like us, mobilized through Fort Bliss. And for obvious reasons, we could not leave Victory until those guys were physically present on the ground, standing tall in front of the commanders. Initially, we had been informed that they had been delayed at Bliss—on the order of one to two weeks, and the anticipation was agony. I caught only a splinter of the emotion that extended combat units must have experienced when, believing that they were to go home in just weeks, were told that they would be staying additional months. But word had finally come down through the Brigade S1 that the replacement docs had arrived in Kuwait and were just waiting on their flight north; there would be no convoy for them!

I had written every possible name, scheduled event, and building location on the dry erase panel lining my trailer door for 1ˢᵗ Battalion's new doc, hoping that it might ease his transition some. With all of my gear crammed back into those green duffels, and with an entire footlocker of stuff already shipped home, I had fallen asleep one last night in the shadow of war. It is no mystery as to why I awoke long before the alarm the following morning. Forty degrees were complemented by gusty rain showers that made it feel like 20, but it was 70 and sunshine to me. Our S1 guys checked in with Brigade to verify that my replacement had indeed bedded down the night before at the Brigade TMC. I had about an hour before they would give me a ride across Victory to BIAP and the flight south.

An hour was just enough time to make one final swing through the Battalion staff and give my final goodbyes. There were a lot of hugs, a lot of back-slaps, a lot of not-suitable-for-printing expressions of envy. My last stop was at the aid station—recently relocated to a large tent facility at the rear of our area. I entered the tent to a chorus of drips: flaws in the cloth "roof" that were being identified by the rain. Jeff McCorcle was positioning buckets around the floors to address the problem. He stood and asked simply, "So, this is it?" As we hugged, I admonished him to keep his head down and not do anything stupid. He promised to comply. I hoped that he meant it.

CPT Lance Magee and one of his NCOs, SGT Toby Teague, were waiting in a humvee for me as I rounded the corner to the battalion TOC. Lance had offered to accompany me to the airfield and make sure that I didn't fall victim to any bureaucratic snags in securing a seat out. The airfield was some 20 minutes across Victory and was an Air Force-operated entity separate from BIAP proper. With the amount of personnel going in and out of such a large base, the air traffic was decidedly busy. There was no big terminal, no skycap—just a dry erase schedule board and a lot of anticipation. At the time of my departure, the 1st Cavalry Division was drawing down its forces, with replacements coming in from the 3rd

Infantry Division out of Fort Benning. The word we had been hearing was that 3rd ID was delaying a lot of folks coming into Baghdad because of their priority status, and that flights north from Kuwait, not south, were at a premium. I was clearly traveling on the correct end of the directional scale. The next flight to Ali Al Saleem Airbase in Kuwait was about an hour away, and with my name on the manifest, my two gracious escorts bade me farewell—after I was unable to locate any stowaway room for them in my luggage. I could've hardly known those guys before, but because of what they had just done for me, they will always be personal heroes. Incredibly, the minutes zipped by quickly, and I was soon out on the tarmac in the manifest line. Kevlar and IBA were donned. Earplugs were jammed deep. Our flight had landed and was offering up its contribution to the war. They all solemnly walked past us along a painted yellow line that we would soon follow. I could only have imagined what they must have been thinking, but I do know what would've been going through *my* mind: "One day, I will be in *that* line."

The transport plane we boarded was no luxury 747. Where there were windows, they were blacked out. The "seats" were seatbelt macramé buckets arranged in parallel lines around the luggage, which had been secured in piles in the center of the cabin. We were instructed to keep our earplugs in place as the engines started. The rear hatch was raised from the concrete, pinching out my last views of Iraq. Without any visibility, our only perception was now the sense of motion as the plane taxied down the runway. I felt no dread of the tactical takeoff that would cork-screw nauseatingly upward in an attempt to avoid a shoulder-fired missile. All the other soldiers and I were focusing on was the anticipation of that first moment of weightlessness as the tires lifted from the runway. Faster...faster...almost...finally! Applause and cheers erupted throughout the cabin—audible even through the roar of the jet engines and the earplugs. I was on my way home.

Eleven

A Civilian Again

—◦◦◦◦—

We left Camp Doha, Kuwait through the same expansive room in which we had been briefed on the Rules of Engagement months before. In a way, it seemed almost as if I had time warped right back to this very spot where I had "swiped in" in October—time warped through a whole truckload of life experience. We were given our second briefing since just prior to our departure from Victory, on the reentry adjustment experience back to civilian life. With so many incidents involving domestic violence and suicide among returning veterans, the Department of Defense had become aggressively involved in prevention of any further tragedies. While it was certainly true that all soldiers desired to be with their families again, some sociological phenomena were also true. Children, especially small ones, may take time to warm up to a parent who has been absent for a long time. Wives who had been successfully running the family without their husbands would not likely appreciate authoritarian advice on household management upon walking in the door. And the instant return of intimacy could not always be guaranteed.

We passed through customs in Kuwait in a building adorned by a relocated bust of Saddam. I was surprised some crafty soldier had not draped a "We hope you enjoyed your time with us in Iraq!" sign around his neck. In customs, we were required to empty *every* item that had been sat on, jammed, and compacted into those green duffel bags. Apparently, in an inspired effort to impress his buddies back home, some fellow Southerner had previously tried to pack a few grenades in with his socks and toothbrush. (He did *not* get home on time.) Most of the other common items considered contraband were fake Rolex watches, Cuban cigars, and hookahs: prizes of the local bazaars and hajji marts. Amazingly, I was able to somehow re-cram all of my junk back into the bags after clearing, and we were finally set to board the plane west to Germany. This one was thankfully a commercial airliner, similar to the one we had ridden over on, and each of the amenities was welcomed. Carpet, upholstered seats, and food served by a means other than a line were things that we had all forgotten over the last months but were glad to quickly re-embrace.

As the flight attendant plodded through the obligatory pre-flight warnings, I peered around at the guys with whom I would be heading back to the New World. Unlike the trip over, where nervous energy was driving an incessant hum of meaningless small talk, except for the "...should there be a sudden drop in cabin pressure..." this plane was silent. And it wasn't because the men were already asleep. Each was staring ahead, consumed in a deep, blissful introspection. While we were all still physically taxiing down a runway in Kuwait City, in truth, we were already living in a future moment: the first hug, the first kiss, the first "Welcome home!" The engines revved, the wheels went up, and we literally...flew off into the sunset.

As before, there was a rather short stop in Germany—short, as in enough time to shave, drink a little coffee from the USO volunteers, and get back on the plane to chase the sun again. In spite of the tremor of anticipation, I was able to get a few hours of sleep in the gentle assurance that each second carried us further westward. The darkness of the East gradually melted into the earliest vestiges of a new dawn in the West, and with a lemony steamed cloth from the flight attendant, we were flying over America's coastline. Touchdown would be in Dallas, enroute to El Paso for our demobilization processing back at Fort Bliss.

As we touched down on blessed American soil, the flight attendant came over the intercom to officially welcome us to the United States of America. She let us know that the airport fire department had flanked two engines at the end of the runway to spray crossed arcs over the plane—providing a ceremonial gateway home. As promised, the high-powered jets of water fired as we taxied up to them, to the applause of everyone in the plane. It was quite a reception. And if that weren't enough, coming off of the jetway, we could all hear a cacophony of cheers and applause brewing at the end. The USO had struck again. This time, instead of ginger snaps and coffee at 2am, it was a receiving line of veterans and retired service members.

Each was decked out in their own custom uniform that gave some description of how they had served. They donned hats and vests that indicated service in wars as far back as WWII and Korea, all the way to the Gulf War. And each was cheering and clapping with the same vigor as if they were in the stands for kickoff at the Super Bowl. There were hugs and handshakes all around, with showers of "Welcome home, son," and "We're proud of you!"

I could only think of one thing, and it unfortunately dwarfed my gratitude: I stank. Since leaving Baghdad what seemed like days earlier, I had been decidedly separated from my luggage, and, well, it was obvious. I guess it had only been masked by the unanimity of everyone else's stench on the plane, but we were now entering the world of the bathed. As I was hugged by the first two of those unfortunate people, I just hoped that their patriotism would allow them to overlook the offense!

Leaving the jetway, we were marshaled into another security clearance area to once again ensure that no one was toting any contraband military equipment or weapons. The officer at the head of the line into the metal detector told us to be prepared to remove our blouse, belt, and possibly our boots.

This sent a chill through me, as I was hyperaware of the crustiness of the military issue wool-blend socks that I had been sweating in since leaving Victory. Should I have been required to remove those boots, I am quite sure that hazardous material alarms would have sounded throughout the terminal. Innocent lives would have been lost. Once again, God's favor was upon me. I traversed the metal detector. No beep. If the people around me could have only known how they had been spared!

And so it was another trip to Fort Bliss — this time to complete the demobilization process prescribed by the Army. Despite my dread of this as a tedious delay in my return home, I would later learn of its deep importance. The primary objective of the "demob" is to assure the physical and psychological well-being of the soldiers, prior to their release from active duty. Should there be an issue related to the deployment, the military rightly views rehabilitation as a manifest responsibility to the service member.

Once at Bliss, I teamed up with John Miller and a couple other guys I mobilized with three months earlier. We were starved for the comforts of the Western world, and waived the open bay quarters for a hotel on post. One of the guys rented a van so we could shuffle between the various stops on our demob checklist without having to wait on Army buses. It ended up being a fabulous arrangement. In just two days' time, we reverse-navigated the same lines we waited in forever the first time. With signatures on papers that certified our physical and mental well-being, we raced to the travel office. Plane tickets were printed. I would be home the next day.

I immediately called Melissa to let her know about my arrival time. I had two reasons for doing this. One, of course, was because I needed a ride home. Another was equally selfish. Because of the close proximity of the airport to our home, Melissa typically left to pick up arrivals at the very last minute. The arrival (usually me) would often have time to hit the restroom, procure luggage, eat a sandwich, and be waiting on the curb for her to pass through. I formed rather cinematic plans for my arrival, thinking that I would run down the tarmac into the terminal into the open arms of my wife and daughters. I figured it would be decidedly un-cinematic to dash into the terminal with a great big "TA-DA" ... and the only person there would be the baggage attendant.

Melissa assured me that she and the girls would indeed be there—early. I boarded the airplane from Houston to Alexandria feeling as if I had just drunk a case of Red Bull. I think I could have probably pushed the plane home on nervous energy alone. Takeoff, cruising altitude, and initial descent were one swift motion, in my recollection. The familiar terrain of home materialized through the wispy clouds. It was velvety green, carved with scattered creeks and lakes. There was not a speck of sand or rock to be found, and I could not be happier for the lack thereof. And there, in the distance, grew a strip of runway.

I do not remember the thump of the tires against the asphalt. Nor do I recall the welcome of the flight attendant to Alexandria, Louisiana. Given that

Alexandria's airport was much smaller at the time and was not equipped with jetways, passengers were relegated to a march down the flight of stairs from the plane and across the tarmac. What this meant was that people in the terminal had full view of passengers during this whole time—for better or for worse. What I did recall of that moment was skipping the final step from the plane to the concrete, and with all of the pent-up passion born by three months of separation, I began my run to the terminal.

In my head, I was playing Rachel Portman's "Homer Returns to the Orphanage," from *The Cider House Rules*—one of those songs I played under the Baghdad stars while I dreamed of home. I dodged passengers who managed to make it off the plane before me, praying that I wouldn't somehow tangle up in some poor old lady's carry-on luggage—and praying that Melissa had made it to the airport on time. The nearer I came to the end of those 50 yards, the faster my pace became. I reached the right-hand turn to the terminal: just a few more feet to a pair of tinted automatic doors. Had they not opened at that moment, I am quite sure that I would have busted right through that glass.

Thankfully, my glass-busting capabilities were left untested as the doors parted. There, in the middle of a blurred crowd were three faces—two little ones partially obscured by pieces of poster board. My hands flew up, and out came some kind of a primal "wahoo!" followed by a familiar sweet voice, "Go get him!" I dropped my laptop case and squatted to the floor to embrace my daughters, who were charging for me at full speed. My squat instantly became a "sit," as their combined momentum was a little more than I expected. And so I sat there, butt on the floor, with Grayson in one hand and Avery in the other, wrapped in the sustained hug and kiss fest that I had longed for.

When they finally allowed me up, there was my precious wife, and a sustained embrace and kiss that made my arrival official. Welcoming me with Melissa and the girls was a crowd of our friends and their kids with their sweet little hero posters. After a warm string of handshakes and hugs, I felt a tap on my back and turned to see the now-familiar features of what appeared to be a middle-aged Middle Eastern man. Behind him was a group of similar-appearing guys with their eyes riveted on me—all were smiling, some looked as if they might have actually had tears welling in their eyes. The man placed his right hand over his heart and proceeded to explain to me that they were all Iraqis on their way to Fort Polk to provide cultural training to deploying Army units. He and his companions then hugged me and thanked me for bringing freedom to their country. It was the most gratifying and unexpected thing I could have expected to find in that terminal. In the end, I could not have *scripted* a better welcome home. It was better than cinematic.

Twelve

Category Five

———— ~~~ ————

The first few days back home were an extended ticker tape parade as I returned to instant American hero status. The local newspaper had its own feature, the health magazine at Rapides Hospital carried a full-page article with photos, and I was peppered with invitations to my own speaker's circuit. After one Rotary Club and two Lions Club invitations, I could almost give the speech on autopilot. I opened with the details of my entry into the military and proceeded to our journey from Kuwait to Baghdad, and on through to my arrival home. The questions that followed at those meetings were of a predictable pattern from nearly everyone I later encountered. Many of them should have been fielded to the Secretary of Defense or one of the Joint Chiefs:

"Do you think we're doing any good over there?"

"Are the Iraqis glad that we're there?"

"How much longer do you think we're gonna have to be over there?"

"Were you ever scared?"

Or my personal favorite and most common request:

"So, what was it like?"

But at the end of those speeches, I was always approached by attendees who also happened to be fellow veterans. Over a firm handshake, they related their own experience in the Pacific, Korea, or Vietnam, noting how similar it had been to my own—and also how completely different. Some were welcomed home as heroes as I had been. Others, sadly, were not.

Initially, I was flattered at the level of interest in my experiences and did everything I could to maintain my enthusiasm in relating the details. By then, there were few Americans who were not affected in some way by the burden of the War, and most were hungry for insight into its progress. With sons and daughters deployed and acquaintances injured or worse, there was a ubiquitous desire for information beyond the scope of network news. I made a strenuous effort to fill in the gaps positively—to relate stories of schools being built and votes being cast, rather than IEDs and casualties. People were always grateful for the truth.

In a practical sense, my transition back to civilian life was a quick one. As is the case with many deployed reservists and guardsmen, time spent on active duty is time spent away from a primary source of income. And while my practice had grown to a healthy size, the return of a pre-deployment revenue stream would take months to realize. During deployment, military personnel are protected from the financial impact of revenue interruption by the Servicemembers Civil Relief Act. This important piece of legislation, dating back to World War II, shields the service member from collection and eviction, in addition to reducing interest rates on some forms of debt. This makes the deployment period bearable. The post-deployment phase, with the removal of the SCRA's protection, is the rough part.

The remedy for me was contract emergency work—and a lot of it—beginning my very first weekend back home. For the next nine months, at least two full weekends, in addition to my weekends on call with my practice, were spent in the emergency room at the LaSalle General Hospital in Jena, Louisiana. I started at 6:00pm on Friday afternoon and trucked on through 6:00am Monday morning, when I headed back to my day job. Fortunately, the work came in spurts, and I was able to grab sleep in between. Despite the fact that LaSalle was a small community hospital in a rural setting, its service area was fairly broad. And the variety of problems that walked—or rolled— through the doors of that ER was equally broad. From car accidents to respiratory arrest to fishhooks in the finger, a little bit of everything was represented. And while I had been as comfortable as I could be with scary things like that before my deployment, I found myself even more assured afterward. After the awful things that I had been front-row witness to in Iraq, the worst Jena could offer seemed tame. At least I was grateful for that. Yet the continued time away from home—after already having been away—was less than easy. I had been gone, and they were understandably ready for me to be back, but the contract work allowed us to keep the lights on until things picked back up at the office.

For all of its downside, the emergency work was a tremendous practice builder. As is all too often the case in emergency departments throughout America, many patients who show up in the ER have no primary care physician. It was a terrific opportunity to meet hundreds of such people at a point when they suddenly realized that need. With time, more and more of them started making the 40-minute drive from Jena to see me at the Brian Clinic. I considered it a powerful affirmation of the care I gave them, and was honored at their trust. Even today, many of those folks are my very dearest patients.

By the spring of 2005, I regrettably found myself fatigued by the inquiry into my war experience. The attention that was initially flattering had grown to be burdensome. And while I wanted to slip on my lab coat and resume the role of Dr. Jonathan Hunter, people were still seeing desert camouflage through the white. There were few occasions where I entered an exam room, and my "Good morning! How are you doing? How's the blood pressure?" was answered with an "It's been good, doc." More typical those days were wide-eyed patients who rose to their feet as I opened the door—like they were witnessing the resurrection of Lazarus. The "Man, am I glad to see you back in one piece!" was then often followed by the same interrogatory that had been taking place since the day of my return. Every friend. Every pharmaceutical representative. Every patient: all wanting answers to the same questions. Some answers were easy. Others, I still don't have the answers for.

As a family physician, many of my patients are young men. Some are in school. Some are working. Others are just starting families. The problems they bring to my office are not always runny noses and poison ivy. The stresses inherent to this phase of life are often profound, and the effect can blight the mental as well as the physical. During those first months back in civilian practice, I found myself still viewing many of them through the eyes of a military physician—and it was nearly always a good thing. In a New Age Pop culture, where emphasis continues to direct focus inward, I became confident in combining conventional medicine with a call to the outward. Any doctor can write a prescription for Prozac and recommend the latest "Discovering a Better You" book on the *New York Times* bestseller list. Lessons I learned in Iraq about stress management, the prioritization of family, and the preeminence of God proved to be dramatic assets. And I became able to impart them with absolute credibility.

By August of 2005, the 256th Brigade was finally making its way home from Iraq. I was just delighted to know that those guys I had left so many months earlier were once again home with their families. Thirty-two of them, however, were not reunited.

Toward the end of a sweltering August, weather reports surfaced on radio and television about a hurricane that had been birthed in the Caribbean. As it barreled toward the Gulf of Mexico, anxiety along

159

the coast heightened. I recalled a talk show I listened to on WWL radio years earlier, while we were still living in New Orleans. Referencing a hurricane that was at that time threatening the Gulf, host Andre Trevine declared to a caller that the city's worst scenario would be a Category Five storm heading up the mouth of the Mississippi.

The fear—which we have now realized—was the resulting storm surge would send water flowing over the city's levees. As *this* storm—now named "Katrina"—continued its march toward the Crescent City with Category Four status, Mayor Ray Nagin issued an unprecedented mandatory evacuation. Claiming it to be the "storm that most of us have long feared," (Staff Writer. *"Katrina Heads for New Orleans." Fox News/Associated Press. August 29, 2005*) he called for New Orleanans to flee the city, and declared the Louisiana Superdome a shelter of last resort. Fear became reality on August 29th.

As the wrath of Katrina's wind and rain bludgeoned the Gulf Coast, the now infamous levees surrounding New Orleans failed, and Lake Ponchartrain poured into the city. Numbed by the near-misses of prior hurricane seasons, many New Orleanans chose to ride Katrina out as they had her predecessors. All Americans are now familiar with the result. Many who ignored the warnings drowned where they stayed. Some were swept away during a panicked escape. And others fled to the Superdome as Katrina's fury rose about them.

The days that followed were a sad dissertation in logistical failure: failure of people to evacuate when warned, failure of relief supplies to reach these non-evacuees, and failure of transportation assets to remove them from some of the most desperate circumstances our country has ever witnessed. Overnight, the old city I grew to love over four years morphed into a soaking pit of human depravity. Streets like Claiborne, Gravier, and Tulane Avenue, upon which I walked countless times, were smothered under four feet of toxic gumbo that spread all the way to the French Quarter.

And while the relief efforts that eventually materialized displayed Americans at their finest, the lawlessness that developed afterward was quite the opposite. Looting, theft, and violence became rampant and were broadcast all over network news. Law enforcement officials who remained behind were instantly overwhelmed and incapable of maintaining control. Enter the military.

Under the command of a Pattonesque Lieutenant General named Russel Honoré—himself a Creole from south Louisiana—troops flooded the streets just as the water had days earlier. It was the perfect answer. Many of the 256 Brigade's soldiers hardly stepped out of their return flights when they were called to service in New Orleans. They were rock-hard, battle-seasoned, and—most of all—very ready to be home. In short, they put up with very little. The rumor spread quickly among those wishing to take advantage of the situation in the city: *do not mess with the guys in the desert camo uniforms.* Of note, my friend LTC John Miller coordinated much of the medical relief effort for the Louisiana National

Guard in the days after the storm, and was awarded the state's highest decoration for a guardsman.

My first Katrina summons came on a Monday night with a call from Greg Brian's brother, Francis. Francis was Rapides Hospital's Vice President for Medical Affairs and had been notified that a convoy of buses from New Orleans was soon to arrive in Alexandria. This was no charter bus with tourists headed for the casino. These buses were packed with residents of a nursing facility from within the city. There was no communication with the buses except for the spotty third-hand accounts from the Red Cross agents, and thus no way to know the condition of the occupants. Francis could only assume the worst and call for help.

Fifteen minutes later, I piled into the surgery lounge with the other enlistees. Nearly all specialties were represented—even the pathologists! We were warned that anything might be on that bus and to be prepared accordingly. Some guy with a Red Cross shirt and a walkie-talkie ducked into the room to let us know that the bus had arrived at the rear of the ER, and we all headed that direction.

Thank God, the bus that came to us was not the hearse that pulled into other facilities. The occupants were mostly little old people who needed some water and air-conditioning. A few were dealing with minor infections of one kind or another. Others, "blessed" by the cloud of Alzheimer's, had no idea of the trauma they just escaped. Two patients—in the rear of the bus—were covered with blankets. For them, it was all just too much.

By the time I got the call from the Guard, things had largely calmed. But nothing could prepare me for the firsthand observance of Katrina's stamp on New Orleans. One drive up West End Blvd. and Canal St. said it all. Mildewed shells of homes spray painted with the infamous FEMA "X" were the norm. Clusters of mud-caked, flooded-out cars were simply abandoned under the I-10 overpasses. Canal St. shops—even those that managed to reopen—were all tattooed with a shockingly high horizontal yellow smudge across their front. Old Charity Hospital, deemed structurally unsafe after the storm, was—for the first time—dark, quiet, and boarded up with plywood over its massive brass front doors. Depressing? Yes.

Instead of caring for storm victims, I looked after the soldiers of Operation Crescent Guard and Task Force Gator: the Louisiana's National Guard's effort to bolster the splintered remnant of the New Orleans Police Department. Housed in a troop medical clinic at Belle Chase Naval Air Station on the West Bank, I took care of the men and women who were charged with taking care of everybody else. Their stories were, well, incredible.

Over conversations about their cough or staphylococcal skin infection, I heard the tales of the streets: both during and after the storm. One 32-year-old staff sergeant was actually working at the Louisiana National Guard's headquarters at Jackson Barracks— just a stone's throw from downtown New Orleans. He sheltered in the dining facility along with other soldiers at the time of Katrina's landfall, on through to the levy breach. With a downcast, blunt stare and the most sober inflection, he recounted the roar of the wind and rain against the roof. And then—as they all did—the focus turned to the water.

Not in terms of hours, but in minutes, the levels rose from inches to feet. His gaze fixed to the tile floor of the exam room when he recounted the bloated corpses floating in the streets and elderly people dying in the Morial Convention Center. And it fell upon him and his comrades to attempt to derive some semblance of order in a place where there was a complete absence of it. I did not hear anything to compare, even at Camp Victory. They were the men and women who were responsible for New Orleans not morphing into a Dodge City in the weeks after her greatest tragedy. Seven-days-a-week, twenty-four-hours-a-day, in sand-colored humvees mounted with blue flashers—keeping gangs and drug dealers from rooting in what had become virgin turf.

Subtract Bourbon Street and replace the statues of Andrew Jackson and Robert E. Lee with Saddam Hussein, and post-Katrina New Orleans was not too different from Baghdad. Both were cities that— admittedly for quite dissimilar reasons—experienced a complete disruption of order. Both were home to a citizenry that grew pathologically dependent on the government provision of basic needs. One was a victim of tyranny. The other was a victim of millibars. In the end, both descended into a chaos that was pounced upon by predatory outlaws. And in the end, both were hefted off the precipice by the arm of the United States military.

Thirteen

Thank You, Lord

—◁◁◁▷▷▷—

Not long after my return from overseas, I began seeing our pastor, Brother Jim Spencer, as a patient. Bro. Jim was our pastor at Kingsville Pastor Church since our college days. Prior to that, he was even Melissa's family's pastor at Comite Baptist Church in Baton Rouge. He was at the hospital when she was born, and he always reminded me that she really belonged to him. So it was fitting that he greeted us at the altar in June of 1995. We loved him—as much as a couple could love a pastor.

And so I was honored the day he cornered me after a Wednesday night prayer meeting to let me know affirmatively, "I'm gonna come see ya'." Bro. Jim was always a bear of a man, with what seemed to be an 18-inch neck and fingers that looked like the handles of a post hole digger. He grappled me in hugs where I smothered in necktie and Brut cologne.

He had undergone cardiac bypass surgery years earlier and lost a great deal of weight afterward—and it was a good thing. But before my departure to Iraq, he seemed to be thinning beyond this healthy slim-down. My first Sunday back at church following my return, with my first glance of him in several months, I leaned over to Melissa and whispered, "Something's wrong with him." His face had grown pale and gaunt. Skin folds dangled below his chin, and I observed a never-before-seen gap between his shirt collar and that thick neck.

A week later, he appeared on my schedule, and I found his new chart hanging from my third exam room at the end of the hall. That morning, he happened to be wearing a close-fitting golf shirt that served only to amplify his condition—whatever it was. His crown of white hair and sterling blue eyes were the only unchanged aspects of his appearance. Everything else was showing signs of some hidden menace. After another one of those hugs—albeit a less robust one, he began relating the details of his "just not feeling well" over the past several months. Symptoms he initially believed were allergy-related did not go away, even after aggressive mold abatement was done in his church office. He continued to be fatigued, continued to lose weight, and continued to suffer from pain in his shoulder that interfered with his fishing cast. And most concerning to me: he had "this durn cough."

In ten minutes, he was on his way across the street to the outpatient center for a chest x-ray. And in two hours, I had the report. Two nodules were visible in his left lung. When I called him on his cell phone to let him know that the x-ray was abnormal, he was completely accepting of the need for the CT scan of his chest. After Myranda arranged the CT, he requested that we call him on his cell or at the office; *he* wanted to be the one breaking any potential bad news to his precious wife, Faye.

Five days later, the CT report came across our fax machine. Judging from the sheer amount of text on the two-pages, I figured the news would not be good. It wasn't. It was devastating. The nodules initially picked up on the chest x-ray were apparently metastatic spread from a hulking ten-centimeter mass in his left kidney. There was evidence of spread in both lungs, the lymph nodes of his chest, and one of his spinal vertebrae—hence the shoulder pain.

In the short course of my medical career to that point, I have delivered a lot of bad news to patients and their families. Initially, like most physicians, I found choosing the right words very tough. We are trained to be diplomatic but also—most importantly—to be honest and frank. Euphemisms and false optimism do nothing more than foster the denial that typically comes with the delivery of such a diagnosis. I also worried about their reaction: would they blame me? Would they doubt my assessment? Would they become so emotional that I would be unable to assuage them? With time and, unfortunately, more experience, doctors gradually become more comfortable with this scenario. They gradually gravitate toward wording that walks the tightrope of comfort and truth. And in doing so, they can maintain just enough professional detachment to not be affected by the gravity of the situation. That was all out the window with Brother Jim.

Not even as a wet-behind-the-ears intern could I ever remember being so gripped at the prospect giving a patient bad news. With heart racing and palms drenched, I dialed the number to the church office. The secretary said that he already left for the day. I tried the cell phone. No answer. I had one option remaining. I dialed the house.

When Faye's sweet little voice answered, I didn't know if I could keep it together. Somehow, I managed to muscle out a fake, "Hey, Mrs. Faye! Where's that rascal?"

"Hey, Jonathan. Let me get him for you."

An eternal pause.

Then, that familiar husky voice, "Hey, pal. How was it?"

"It's bad, brother."

I then proceeded to explain the findings of the CT scan to him as he listened in silence. When I was finished, he cut right to The Question: "How long?"

"I've been made a fool of before with predictions," I explained to him, "but I don't see this going past six months."

The extent of the spread was just already too extreme. He accepted the news in silence.

"What do we do next?" he inquired, and I began detailing my plan to get him in immediately with a local oncologist.

Two days later, he was evaluated and plans were made for a biopsy of the mass, as well as a referral to the M.D. Anderson Cancer Center in Houston.

The biopsy did in fact confirm that Brother Jim was suffering from renal cell carcinoma. And so began his series of trips to and from Houston. Initially, he was started on a two-drug experimental protocol that thankfully provided some initial regression of his disease. With this glimmer of hope, surgery was then performed to remove the mass as well as the affected kidney. Yet despite all of this medical heroism, the cancer inevitably advanced. His weight continued to fall. His once booming preacher's voice grew weak and raspy. By February of 2006, he had endured about all that he could.

Three years earlier, Brother Jim declared to me in the middle of one of his hugs that he and I needed to go fishing. That was not a tall order. I loved to fish, and I had never been on the water with him; it sounded great to me. I met him at 6:00 on a Tuesday morning at his house. As I turned the corner onto his street, I could see that his maroon pickup was staged in the driveway: facing outward with the boat behind. He greeted me with a handshake and a stainless steel thermos mug of coffee. I hopped in the cab and threw on my seat-belt when he paused to pray—something I admit I had never done before a fishing trip. He thanked God for the day and for me and my friendship. He didn't even pray for a big bass. It was all about gratitude. With an amen, we were off to Cane River.

The weather could not have been more ideal on that summer morning: 75 degrees and a cloudless sky with just the slightest occasional breeze. As we moved down what was obviously a familiar stretch of the river to him, he occasionally called out the depth of the water (he was never off by more than a foot). Only I could see the actual depth on the boat's monitor, and he was letting me know that he had fished this water a few times before. In the end, I honestly don't remember if we even caught fish that day. What I do remember is that about every 15 minutes, he would cast his bait with a "Thank you, Lord." It wasn't loud enough for it to have been for my benefit. It was just between him and God—and the largemouth bass.

On February 28, 2006, Jim Spencer was at home with his family—where he wanted to be. With one final earthly breath, he stepped across another river to meet the Savior to whom he had devoted his life. My pastor and dear friend—healed completely. Thank you, Lord.

Fourteen

Wounded Warriors

On August 4, 2006, I received an email from the Louisiana National Guard, informing me of my impending transfer from 1st Battalion to the Medical Command at Camp Beauregard in Pineville. Instead of being a doctor for a combat unit, I would be involved in certifying medical readiness for soldiers throughout the state. I would miss the guys with whom I had been through so much, but this was a welcome change. The drills were closer to home, and I would be seeing another side of medical care within the Guard. It was a good thing. But I felt differently about the bottom of the email.

CW4 Charlene Adams concluded the transfer notice with this: "It looks like you will be tasked for another 90 day rotation in CONUS from March-May 2007."

Translation: *You are being deployed again, but you're not going to go to Iraq this time.*

I wish I could say that I embraced this news with eager anticipation of further service to my country. I didn't. As that strange prickly heat sizzled my face, I was instantly reminded of the pains of the last such notification. At that point, the continent upon which I would serve was of less consequence. What mattered most was one thing: separation. With or without IEDs and Islamic extremists, it was a promise of 90 days of no Melissa, Grayson, or Avery.

I soon learned that during this second deployment, I would be the medical officer for the Community Based Healthcare Organization (CBHCO) of Alabama. The CBHCO was a new program for the Army born out of a similar such initiative dating back to WWII. National Guard and Reserve soldiers returning from deployments frequently suffer from injuries or illnesses that are incurred during their time of service. Traditionally, they were cared for at a large military treatment facility like Walter Reed Army Medical Center in Washington, where they could be housed for weeks. And at times—as most Americans are now aware—the facilities in which they were housed were somewhat less than adequate. Moreover, during this whole protracted recuperation, these same soldiers were decidedly *not* at home. Enter the CBHCO.

Put simply, soldiers accepted into the CBHCO are sent home to receive care through civilian providers. They remain on active duty orders and report daily to a local armory where they have a job commensurate with their capabilities, with the entire process overseen by a central, regionally located command.

Alabama's CBHCO had initially been located in Birmingham, but moved to Redstone Arsenal in Huntsville in November of 2006. Its staff directed the care of soldiers from Alabama, Tennessee, Kentucky, and Mississippi.

As medical officer, I approved soldiers' initial suitability for the program, making sure that their condition was a proper fit for the CBHCO model. Beyond that, progress is tracked weekly to then eventually decide an end point when "maximal medical benefit" has been achieved. Soldiers are then either released from active duty back to their Guard or reserve units, or they begin the medical discharge process.

After the 24-7 public relations debacle that had fixed on Walter Reed, the Army became earnestly invested in the success of the CBHCO. After the banner headlines implying that the military was not adequately caring for its wounded, senior officers were axed, and the message sent was clear: *the Army will take care of its wounded.* I joined this initiative at a time of acute Pentagon-level interest.

At least with this deployment, I was only an eight-hour drive from home, so this departure was far different emotionally from its predecessor. And as an added bonus, my mobilization processing was ordered at Fort Benning, Georgia instead of the transcontinental, go-way-out-west-to-come-way-back-east trek that would have been Fort Bliss. This was a relatively short drive to Columbus, Georgia to punch in, followed by an even shorter jaunt to Huntsville.

I was admittedly excited to see Fort Benning. After learning of the exploits of Major Dick Winters and his Band of Brothers, I was anxious to lay eyes on the storied installation where so many American heroes were trained. It did not disappoint. Tucked in the piney woods of southwest Georgia, Benning is an eclectic mix of the Army's grandest tradition and its most modern destructive might. Driving down its streets and seeing signs like "Home of the Infantry" and "Rock of the Marne" are a humbling experience for any American soldier. I felt honored to be there.

The CRC was set up similarly to its counterpart at Fort Bliss. Individuals rather than whole units were processed, pronounced fit for deployment, and sent all over God's earth. The first such individual I got to know would become one of the most memorable of my military experience.

As I sat alone at one of the long tables in the CRC dining facility, I was approached by a 70-something year-old gentleman in woodland camo with an outstretched meal tray. "May I join you?" he inquired in exactingly precise English. I obliged, and so began my introduction to Colonel Everett Spees.

After the introductions, the colonel launched a salvo of questions over his dinner; my name, schooling, family, medical practice, and military experience were all covered. Then he returned the favor. Colonel Spees was a cardiothoracic surgeon from Boulder, Colorado, who entered the Army a *long* time ago—so long that his date of rank as a colonel was 1972! On top of all that, he possessed a PhD in microbiology, which he incorporated into his research practice as a military surgeon. And, as if he actually needed something more, he admitted to me that he attended seminary to become an ordained Eucharistic minister. This was a guy who had it all covered: anything from hearts to germs to souls was within his restorative power.

In his capacity as an Army reservist, Colonel Reverend Doctor Spees was a free agent guy the Army called to voluntarily deploy in a particular time of need. And, as one might guess, he usually agreed. After all, how many people with that kind of experience with that list of credentials—and such a willingness to offer them—existed in the country? No literary hyperbole here: over that meatloaf or Salisbury steak or whatever it was, I knew I was seated across from a real-deal American legend.

After three quick days of processing at Benning, Dr. Spees was on a plane to Landstuhl to serve as Chief of Surgical Services, and I was in my Jeep bound for Huntsville. Amazingly, I did not get lost finding the CBHCO headquarters building behind the massive NASA facility also at Redstone. At their morning formation, I was introduced to the staff by the commanding officer, Lieutenant Colonel Rachel Clay. The chief item of business at the formation was an upcoming inspection by Pentagon representatives from the Army's Undersecretary for Manpower and Reserve Affairs: upcoming, as in the next week.

Now, after my cursory study of the basic operation of the CBHCO, I was semi-comfortable with assuming the role of its medical officer. In this case, part of that role was briefing a bunch of guys from the Pentagon—hardly what I could have anticipated. Thankfully, the "briefing" constituted reciting statistics off a series of PowerPoint slides, and any extrapolation was deferred to those who had been there longer than, well, a week. It was just another in a series of reminders that the Army was mightily serious about the success of the CBHCO and was assuring that at its highest command.

I worked closely with Lieutenant Colonel Deborah Davis who was the CBHCO's nurse practitioner from Jackson, Mississippi. To my delight, she had been there for a good while and was well-versed in the intricacy of all of its moving parts. She was wonderfully collegial and did all she could to get me up to speed, both as the medical officer and for the Pentagon briefing. At that time, a review of some of the statistics of soldiers entering the CBHCO was revealing.

Approximately 95% of the principal conditions was orthopedic—largely injured backs, shoulders, and knees. This was certainly no surprise, given the intense combat conditions from which they had come, and was historically consistent with any war. Also common to any war of any era was post-traumatic stress disorder. Whether known as PTSD or "shellshock," the psychological effect of war can obviously be deep and far-reaching. And particularly with the increasing incidence of post-deployment domestic violence and suicide, the military was aggressively invested in the detection and treatment of any such problem. Another common problem was born more out of this particular IED-ridden conflict. "Traumatic brain injury," more commonly considered a concussion, is the result of a blow to the head that can result in long-term cognitive and psychomotor impairment. For veterans of Iraq and Afghanistan, these injuries were typically the result of an IED blast to the vehicle they were occupying.

The visit from the Pentagon staffers confirmed the Army's interest in the welfare of its own. They listened with keen interest to the presentation of the CBHCO staff and seemed delighted to hear from me, given my prior Iraq experience. Most of the group consisted of retired officers and NCOs. They made a career of putting on the uniform and completing the mission, and they did it by looking after other soldiers. The message was clear: *You do whatever it takes to take care of our soldiers.*

Over the next three months, I devoted my professional energies to doing just that. Every week, every enrolled soldier was reviewed by the CBHCO team. I heard from their case manager and platoon sergeant about their progress—or lack thereof. Their doctor visits, therapy sessions, and surgery plans were all reviewed. And in the end, a decision had to be made. Sometimes it was easy. Sometimes it was not.

One of the first guys I had the privilege of doing the initial intake on was a middle-aged Apache helicopter mechanic [obviously someone for whom I held great affection] who was hurt during a recent deployment to Iraq. He was a senior NCO with an injury that required surgery, and he was going to require several weeks of physical therapy. As I sat there with him and LTC Davis, he related his affection for the younger guys he left behind, as well as his passion for the work he was doing over there.

With an unwavering smile, he reiterated a singular request, "Sir, just whatever I need to do, please get me back with my guys."

That was not the only time I would hear that during my time at the CBHCO. Another young infantryman entered the program to recover from a shrapnel injury that he incurred from his *third* IED encounter. Thankfully, it is impossible for most people to imagine what it's like to be blown up once. Even without a resulting injury, the psychological trauma incurred by such an event is not describable, and accounted for countless referrals for PTSD treatment. This guy only left the theater because a piece of scrap metal ripped through a sheet of muscle in his chest wall. And he was ready to go back.

As I drove away from Huntsville after three months, I carried the satisfaction of knowing that my care of the American soldier had come full circle. I was with them where they trained. I was with them where they fought. And I was with them when they returned as wounded warriors. Through it all was a lesson far deeper and more profound than patriotic appreciation. Through their example, I witnessed some of the finest embodiment of resilient determination that a human being can muster. Despite the obstacle: whether it be heat, fatigue, shrapnel, water, hate, pain, grief, disability, or illness…God will allow challenges in us all. It is simply up to us to decide how we will meet them.

In this world you will have trouble. But take heart I have overcome the World.

John 16:33

Fifteen

What Matters Most

I am confident that if a convention of history's greatest physicians was assembled, the pillars of our profession would agree the intangible element that separates good doctors from great ones does not come from a book or a lecture. From Hippocrates to Osler to Debakey, greatness is observed in thoughtful submission rather than pronouncement. In its purest and most noble form, medicine is, after all, about *the patient*. On Canal Street and on Haifa Street. In blue jeans or in digital camouflage. Truth is no respecter of continent or position.

In the end, where there is a physician with this humble deference, there is much more than a doctor. There is the very embodiment of God's healing hand upon this earth.

There is found a healer, a counselor, and a friend.

CPSIA information can be obtained
at www.ICGtesting.com
Printed in the USA
FFOW03n2219200617
36951FF